The Web Was Done by Amateurs

Marco Aiello

The Web Was Done by Amateurs

A Reflection on One of the Largest Collective Systems Ever Engineered

 Springer

Marco Aiello
University of Stuttgart
Stuttgart, Germany

ISBN 978-3-319-90007-0   ISBN 978-3-319-90008-7   (eBook)
https://doi.org/10.1007/978-3-319-90008-7

Library of Congress Control Number: 2018939304

Printed on acid-free paper

This Springer imprint is published by the registered company Springer International Publishing AG part of Springer Nature.
The registered company address is: Gewerbestrasse 11, 6330 Cham, Switzerland

The original version of this book was revised. An correction to this book can be found at https://doi.org/10.1007/978-3-319-90008-7_12

Preface

The field of computer science is so young that sometimes we think of it as history-less, as a set of cutting-edge technologies without a past. This is a crucial mistake. The field might be relatively young, especially when compared with other traditional exact sciences, such as mathematics and physics, but it has a very dense history. A fitting comparison is the life expectancy of a dog vs. that of a human: a year in computer science is equivalent to seven years in other scientific fields. On the one hand, such speed of innovation is exciting and one of computer science's characterizing features; on the other hand, it too often prevents us from reflecting on the history, and consequently we reinvent the wheel.

In my 20 years as a lecturer of computer science, I have noticed that students are often incredibly skilled in the latest technologies but are not able to place them into their historical and societal context. Something like the Web is taken for granted. Occasionally, a student will place the Web's birth in the 1950s. The problem becomes even more evident when they start designing a system for their final project. The intuitions and ideas may be very worthwhile, but often they have been proposed before, unbeknownst to the student. My feeling is that they lack heroes and role models. They lack an Einstein or Fermi to look up to, a Freud or a Jung to place at the origin of their field. This gap is not due to the absence of exceptional computer science founding fathers—and mothers. It is rather that most ignore the origins of a model, an idea, a technique, or a technology. Who invented the Web? When? Who proposed object-oriented programming? Why? Who coined the term Artificial Intelligence? How is it defined? These are questions that Web engineers, software engineers, and Artificial Intelligence students—not to mention the general public—too often cannot answer.

The present book was born with the desire to systematize and fix on paper historical facts about the Web. No, the Web was not born in the 1950s; it is not even 30 years old. Undoubtedly, it has changed our lives, but it has done so in just a few decades. So, how did it manage to become such a central infrastructure of modern society, such a necessary component of our economic and social interactions? How did it evolve from its origin to today? Which competitors, if any, did it have to win over? Who are the heroes behind it? These are some of the questions that the present book addresses. The book also covers the prehistory of the Web so as to better understand its evolution.

Even if it is perhaps obvious, it is still worthwhile to remark that there is an important difference between the Web and the Internet. The Web is an application built over the Internet. It is a system that needs a communication infrastructure to allow users to navigate it and follow a link structure distributed among millions of Web servers. The Internet is such an infrastructure, allowing computers to communicate with each other. The confusion sometimes arises due to the fact that the Web and its companion email are the most successful applications over the Internet. Nevertheless, the Web and the Internet are two distinct systems. The present book is about the Web. It will often refer to the Internet, as the relation between the two is very close indeed, but the book focuses only on the Web.

The book is organized into four parts. *Part I: The Origins* covers the prehistory of the Web. It looks at the technology that preexisted the Web and fostered its birth. It also covers earlier hypertextual systems that have preceded the emergence of the Web. The narrative is historical in nature with many references and quotations from the field's pioneers.

Part II: The Web describes the original Web proposal as defined in 1989 by Tim Berners-Lee and the most relevant technologies associated with it. The presentation is mostly historical in nature.

Part III: The Patches combines the historical reconstruction of the evolution of the Web with a more critical analysis of the original definition and of the necessary changes to the initial design. The presentation has both an historical and an engineering flavor.

Finally, *Part IV: System Engineering* looks at the Web as an engineered infrastructure and reflects on its technical and societal success. The narrative here predominantly takes a system's engineering view, considering the Web as a unique, gigantic case study. There are occasional historical elements and a few considerations with a philosophy of science twist to them.

The book was written with the technological-engaged and knowledge-thirsty reader in mind, ranging from the curious daily Web user to the computer science and engineering student. People with diverse backgrounds

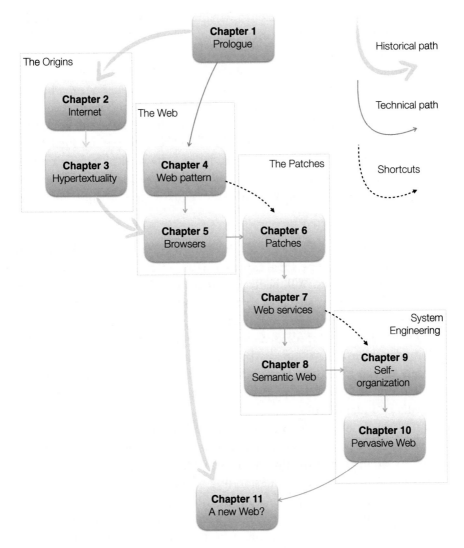

Fig. 1   Possible reading paths

might want to personalize their reading experience. The more historically oriented reader who has less background and interest in computer science should follow the thick, gray arrow on Fig. 1, most notably skipping Part III and optionally going through Part IV. Similarly, those already familiar with the history of the Internet and of the prehistory of the Web can follow the thin, gray line in Fig. 1 and go for the more technical chapters. Two chapters can be considered optional: Chap. 8 on the Semantic Web is slightly more technical than the rest and can be safely skipped. Chapter 5 on Web browsers and their wars has a vintage taste that will appeal to the baby boomers, but may be less relevant to the millennials.

In looking at the history and evolution of the Web, we will encounter many interesting characters and pioneers. A few recur throughout the history and will be often present. The most notable three are Tim Berners-Lee, who invented the Web; Alan Kay, who is one of the founding fathers of computer science and has a strong feeling about the Web (he also inspired the title of the present book); and Ted Nelson, who defined the field of hypertextuality with his pioneering Xanadu system. Could these be the heroes that computer science generations need? For sure they are visionaries to look up to and who will be remembered.

I have based the historical reconstruction presented here on many books, papers, and Web pages. These are all cited throughout the book. I have also employed facts from my personal experience or directly communicated to me by prominent colleagues. Wikipedia has often been the starting point for my research. I did not put references to the Wikipedia entries, though, as they are quite straightforward and I can imagine anybody being able to just input the keywords in the Wikipedia search box. As a sign of my appreciation, I did regularly donate to the Wikipedia Foundation, and I plan to do so again in the future. If you have downloaded this book for free from the Internet, you know, kind of illegally, I do suggest that at least you make a donation to the Wikipedia Foundation, too.

Writing this book has been great fun, and it helped me to reflect on the history of the Web, at times reconstructing facts that were vaguely stored in the back of my mind. I took the liberty of the occasional personal and subjective consideration, based on my understanding of science and technology. Being used to writing objective and unbiased scientific papers, such freedom was new to me and at times inebriating. While the fumes of freedom might have made my style looser than usual, it has never been my intention to offend anyone or put down the hard work of respectable individuals. In fact, there are only good, heroic visionaries in this book, no traces of bad guys—at most, some people who might have misjudged the ugly effects of specific design decisions or who have simply behaved like *amateurs* by ignoring the history of the field to which they were contributing.

Sydney, June 2017   Marco Aiello

Acknowledgements

"The Web Was Done by Amateurs" could not exist without the help of many people. I take this occasion to thank the prominent ones and apologize if I have unintentionally forgotten anyone. First and foremost, I thank Alan Kay for being who he is and for his contributions to our field. Second, I thank Tim Berners-Lee for creating the Web, bringing it to success, and defending its openness ever since. I also thank him for being a physicist.

My internship at Apple's Advanced Technology Group in 1995 was eye opening in many ways. I thank Jim Spohrer for the opportunity and Martin Haeberli for his mentoring while there. Martin is also the one who first pointed me to the "As We May Think" paper of Vannevar Bush cited in Chap. 3, and the "End-to-End Arguments" paper cited in Chap. 9.

After my introduction to the Web, my journey continued with Web services thanks to a suggestion of Fausto Giunchiglia and the introduction to the theme by Mike Papazoglou. I owe them both for this.

Alexander Lazovik has been my first PhD student and the person who has given body, concreteness, and theoretical foundations to many of my intuitions. He has been my most valuable colleague since we first met in 2002. I also thank the many members of the Distributed Systems group at the University of Groningen with whom I collaborated over the years to obtain some of the results mentioned throughout the book.

Matt McEwen has done an incredible job at analyzing the story behind my book and helping me better present the material. I also received many precious suggestions from: Frank Blaauw, Talko Dijkhuis, Laura Fiorini, Heerko Groefsema, Massimo Mecella, Andrea and Gaetano Pagani, Jorge Perez, Azkario Pratama, Rolf Schwitter, and Brian Setz. Any remaining error can only be ascribed to myself.

I am indebted to Alfred Hofmann and Ralf Gerstner from Springer who enthusiastically embraced this book project, not being intimidated by the controversial title. Their professional and dedicated help gave great support and improved the value proposition of the present book.

Hannah Sandoval of PurpleInkPen has acted as my copy editor and has done a wonderful job over the various evolutions of the manuscript. She knows the art of making otherwise convoluted sentences flow.

I have written the present book while on sabbatical leave from the University of Groningen at the Macquarie University of Sydney. I thank both institutions for making this possible and supporting my visit Down Under.

I thank Andrew Binstock and UBM for granting permission to reproduce the entire 2012 interview of Alan Kay.

My parents, Mario and Gigina Aiello, have been two pioneers of computer science and artificial intelligence. This led them to first meet Alan Kay in 1974, and they have had regular contact since. I thank them for having provided genes, inspiration, foundations, and love. Additionally, my mother endured in reading many early drafts of the book. Serves her right for having given birth to yet another computer scientist.

I thank my family for supporting and bearing with me during the book writing process: my children, Maurizio and Aurelia, for being the biggest source of laughter and smiles I have and will ever encounter; my wife, Heike, for supporting all my ideas, no matter how crazy, putting up with my unadjusted sleeping patterns, and being a source of love, tenderness, and many great suggestions on how to make my text more crisp and accessible. The book would have not been possible nor readable without her presence in my life.

Contents

1	**The Web Was Done by Amateurs**	1
	1.1 Text Versus Objects	3
	1.2 The Birth of the Web	4

| **Part I** | **The Origins** | 7 |

2	**The Pacific-Ocean Internet**	9
	2.1 ARPANET	10
	2.2 Comments, Please!	12
	2.3 The Internet	16
	2.4 Why Is It a Natural Resource?	17

3	**Hypermedia Until the Web**	21
	3.1 How We May Think	25
	3.2 The oN-Line System (NLS)	28
	3.3 Xanadu	29
	3.4 HyperCard	32
	3.5 Enquire and the Birth of the Web	33

Part II The Web   39

4 The Original Web Pattern   41
    4.1   Uniform Resource Locator   45
    4.2   HyperText Transfer Protocol   46
    4.3   HyperText Markup Language   48

5 The Browser Lament   51
    5.1   The Browser Is an Application   52
    5.2   Early Browsers   53
    5.3   Netscape   56
    5.4   Microsoft's Internet Explorer   57
    5.5   Google's Chrome   60

Part III The Patches   63

6 Patching the Web   65
    6.1   Patch I: Cookies   66
    6.2   Patch II: Run Anywhere   69
    6.3   Patch III: Scripting   73

7 Patch IV: Web Services   79
    7.1   Securing the Intranet   79
    7.2   Corba and IDLs   80
    7.3   The Magic Triangle   82
    7.4   Service-Oriented Computing   87
    7.5   A Personal Tale: Compose It Now!   89
    7.6   The Patch   92
    7.7   Who's Serving?   93
    7.8   XML Web Services Versus the REST   94
    7.9   Vaporizing Services   95

8 The Unexploited Patch   101
    8.1   The Semantic Gap   102
    8.2   Subsumptions Subsumed by Subsumptions   106
    8.3   The Patch   108

Part IV System Engineering   113

9   The Self-Organizing Web   115
   9.1   The Size and Shape of the Web   116
   9.2   Self-Organization and Complex Networks   119
   9.3   Searching the Web   122
   9.4   Self-Organization, Patching, and the Role of Amateurs   126

10 The Pervasive Future   129
   10.1   Apps   130
   10.2   Web (on the Internet) of Things   133
   10.3   The Web and Artificial Intelligence   136

11 Should a New Web Be Designed?   141

Correction to: The Web Was Done by Amateurs   E1

A   Dr. Dobb's Interview with Alan Kay   145
   A.1   A Note About Dr. Dobb's Journal   145
   A.2   The Interview   146

References   153

Index   161

1

The Web Was Done by Amateurs
A 2012 Reflection of Alan Kay

"The Web was done by Amateurs." This is what Alan Kay told Andrew Binstock in 2012 for a piece that appeared in the *Dr. Dobb's journal,* a magazine popular among programmers and applied computer scientists. In the interview, Kay presented his personal history and his view of computer science. While reading the interview, there was a passage that caught my attention, something that combined controversy and surprise. He stated, "The Internet was done so well that most people think of it as a natural resource like the Pacific Ocean, rather than something that was man-made. When was the last time a technology with a scale like that was so error-free? The Web, in comparison, is a joke. The Web was done by amateurs."[1]

A quote from Alan Kay is just like a good Kubrick movie, much deeper than it appears at first sight and requiring you to view it several times before truly appreciating the cleverness and insightfulness of the scripting and shooting. Initially, I read the quote superficially, but somehow it stayed in my head till one day while I was lecturing about Web programming and illustrating the many ways to share the computational load between client and server, I ended up citing that very last sentence of Kay's to the students. They looked at me puzzled. First, I had to explain who Alan Kay is and recount his many outstanding contributions as, surprisingly for computer science students, most ignored his name. Consequently, I had to explain what most likely originated

---

[1]Even though "The Web was *made* by amateurs" is preferable in English, the book is titled "The Web was *done* by amateurs" to match literally the statement of Alan Kay. His full interview is reproduced in the appendix.

© Springer International Publishing AG, part of Springer Nature 2018
M. Aiello, *The Web Was Done by Amateurs,*
https://doi.org/10.1007/978-3-319-90008-7_1

such a sentence—why he would even say something so trenchant. Finally, I had to argue why that sentence is a fine and compact mélange of insights.

Once home, I read the interview again and slowly realized that I had spent nearly 20 years of my career just working around that original design issue. The Web was done by amateurs who forgot that computers are there to compute, as if they just got carried away by the networking abilities of the Pacific Ocean-Internet. As a computational infrastructure, the Web is ineffective: a scalable cemetery of consistency, and a place full of patches designed to cover the lack of distributed resource availability and data coherence. What is the basic exchange unit on the Web? Loosely formatted text. Not an abstract data object whose behavior is precisely and formally defined. Not a program that can travel across the network and harvest computational resources to carry on its tasks. The Web has been designed to just be a distributed infrastructure for static message exchange and static textual linking. But before I dive into the controversy, let me recall who Alan Kay is.

Alan Curtis Kay was born in Springfield, Massachusetts, on May 17, 1940 [11]. After starting college, he joined the Air Force, where he was assigned to the programming of an IBM 1401, his first exposure to computers. After a few years in the army, he decided to continue his studies at the University of Colorado, earning a degree in mathematics and molecular biology in 1966. He then went to the University of Utah to obtain a PhD in computer science in 1969. During that period he was also exposed to the ARPANET initiative, as his university was among the first nine nodes to be connected to it. In that period, Kay also attended the San Francisco Computer Science conference and was present at the "Mother of All Demos" of Engelbart's NLS system, which we will describe in Sect. 3.2. The system had a profound influence on Kay's vision and subsequent work.

After earning his PhD, Kay moved to the Silicon Valley. He started working on novel programming languages in John McCarthy's Stanford Artificial Intelligence Lab, and in 1971, he joined the Xerox Palo Alto Research Center (PARC). At PARC he worked on objects, graphical interfaces, and inter-networking. In these years, his ideas about the blooming field of computer science became concrete. He designed and implemented one of the first object-oriented programming languages in 1972, SmallTalk, and led the development of a graphic-based personal computer, the Alto, which was the inspiration for the first Apple Macintosh released in 1984.

Kay has received an impressive number of awards, among which is his ACM Turing Award of 2003: computer science's most prestigious prize given yearly to a distinguished contributor to the field and considered the equivalent of the Nobel Prize for the discipline. Similarly to the Nobel, it carries a monetary award of one million dollars.[2] He has also been elected a Fellow of the American Academy of Arts and Sciences, the National Academy of Engineering, and the Royal Society of Arts.

1.1 Text Versus Objects

Say that one wants to add two numbers together. On the Web, one would go to a site known for performing additions, a site found as a result of a Web search. Then one inputs a textual (textual!) form of the desired addition and waits. The server takes the text, interprets it as an addition, uses programming code unknown to the user to add up the numbers, and sends back a long textual page where somewhere therein is a string of text that represents the numeric result sought. This approach, which is the original pattern of the Web, implies sending large bulks of semantically unspecified text which need to be interpreted as an addition, while actually the operation could have been easily done locally, on the computer of the user, had there been programming code downloaded to the client. Even worse, say that now the same user wants to perform 50 additions, or even 500, or thousands. How does one know that the written input text will be interpreted as an addition and that the result is correct? How much network bandwidth is consumed for such simple additions? What if one experiences a temporary disconnection from the server?

The original sin of the Web lies squarely in this way of looking at the node interactions, considering them simple textual exchanges, rather than full computational ones. In the case of an addition, what one would have ideally wanted to do is to send two objects which represent numbers and encapsulate the code for arithmetical operations. Calling the object-defined "addition operation" will result in a new object number: the desired addition value. That object is what one really wants. Not some text possibly representing that object.

I know that this example is a bit extreme, and I am well aware of all alternative ways to add numbers or compute on the Web. I know about cookies, scripts, virtual machines, and dynamic content. I know about JavaScript, SOAP, WSDL, and AJAX; actually, I know these technologies well enough to overview them later in the book. What I argue is that these are all *patches* that have gradually been introduced to solve the original design shortcomings of

---

[2]The Award was created in 1966 with no monetary value. From 2007 to 2014 it was accompanied by a $250,000 award, and thereafter by $1,000,000.

the Web, and they are what most likely forced Alan to say about Wikipedia, "Go to the article on Logo, can you write and execute Logo programs? Are there examples? No. The Wikipedia people didn't even imagine that, in spite of the fact that they're on a computer."

Kay is not attacking Wikipedia. His argument is that a Web page about the functional, programming language Logo has as much Logo running ability as a page about whales. One would like to find a remote container with the ability of understanding Logo statements, receiving Logo programs, and displaying the results on a Logo console or by moving around the Logo turtle.

1.2   The Birth of the Web

There are two answers to the question of who created the Web. The *short* answer is, the physicist Tim Berners-Lee while working at the European Organization for Nuclear Research, CERN. An internal proposal for funding was submitted in 1989 and approved. The core innovation put forward was that of a distributed hypertextual repository and three simple yet very effective technologies: HTML, HTTP, and URLs. The *long* answer is that the Web emerged in a fervent period of computer science research into *hypertextuality*, human-computer interaction, information retrieval, and internetworking. The long answer is what this book is about. In particular, Chap. 3 introduces some of the visionaries who proposed hypertextual systems before the birth of the Web and prepared the grounds for it. Among them, it is worth anticipating here the name of Ted Nelson and his Xanadu project. The project saw its birth in the 1960s, along with Nelson's coining of the term *hypertextuality*. In Xanadu, documents are interlinked with each other, and the notion of a *transclusion* serves the purpose of incorporating text, via hyperlinks, to create new documents as compositions of new and existing text. Interestingly, the proposal considers bidirectional links to trace back the source of incoming pointers and has provisions for copyright payments.

Ted Nelson, a strong and poignant personality, has been openly critical of the Web, though for reasons that are orthogonal to those of Kay. He focuses more on the user perspective and hypertextuality of the Web versus Xanadu, which anticipated the Web by over 20 years. He states, "HTML is precisely what we were trying to PREVENT—ever-breaking links, links going outward only, quotes you can't follow to their origins, no version management, no rights management." Very direct, with occasional traits of a curmudgeon, he also addresses directly the creator of the Web—which Kay explicitly avoids in his own interview. Nelson states, "After all, dumbing down Xanadu sure worked well for Tim Berners-Lee!" The inventor of the Web has not replied directly to the criticism of Nelson, though in his 1999 book about the birth of the Web and its first 10 years of existence, he appears to defend his choices for simplicity over complex design [19]. He states, "When I designed HTML for the Web, I chose to avoid giving it more power than it absolutely needed—a 'principle of least power,' which I have stuck to ever since. I could have used a language like Donald Knuth's TEX, which though it looks like a markup language is in fact a programming language. It would have allowed very fancy typography and all kinds of gimmicks, but there would have been little chance of turning Web pages into anything else. It would allow you to express absolutely anything on the page, but would also have allowed Web pages that could crash, or loop forever."

The exploration of the history prior to the Web and its evolution after its initial introduction is one of the objectives of the present book. The goal is to interpret the criticism of Kay and place Nelson's arguments into perspective, while recognizing the merit and role of the Web in the context of computer science. In fact, there is a natural tension between beautiful designs that too often remain unrealized and simplistic yet effective solutions that the world is eager to embrace. This motif will accompany us throughout the whole book. It is not my goal to resolve such tension, but rather to acknowledge it. The Web is one of the largest collective systems ever engineered, a critical infrastructure of our society, a sociological game changer, a revolutionary business tool. Simply understanding how it started and how it became what it is today, is a goal in itself.

Tim Berners-Lee has surely had to bear with the few critical voices, though this is certainly compensated by the many and well-deserved recognitions he has received through the years. The most remarkable and recent is the 2016 ACM Turing Award. In addition to Tim Berners-Lee and Alan Kay, we will meet many more Turing Award winners while reconstructing the history of the Web, including John McCarthy, Donald Knuth, Edgar Codd, Douglas Engelbart, Vinton G. Cerf, Robert E. Kahn, and Leslie Lamport. Before the Turing Award, Tim Berners-Lee was honored in 2004 with a knightship from the British queen, and was elected a fellow of many prominent academic societies.

In addition to the technical contribution, Tim Berners-Lee stands out for his passion and dedication to defend the openness and fairness of the Web. He has tried to protect his creation from the conquests of many corporations that have been trying to steer the technology in their direction in an attempt to monopolize the fruition of the Web. Chapter 5 will recall some of the epic competitions among the browser makers and how NCSA,

Netscape, Microsoft, and later Google have battled in what are known as the "browser wars." In the early days of the Web, Tim Berners-Lee supported the openness of the technology, and encouraged others to adopt it and build their own interconnected components. Later, he made outstanding efforts toward standardizing all the elements of the Web, in turn, guaranteeing that all parties could participate, irrespective of their economic capabilities and market shares. He is also a fervent advocate of Net neutrality, making sure that all the users and applications get the same fair usage of the Internet and, in turn, the Web. I consider these efforts to be as worthy as the technological invention, if not even more important. In other terms, I would consider a nomination for the Nobel Peace Prize as not too far-fetched given the importance of the Web in information dissemination, education, and fair access to knowledge.

Part I

The Origins

2

The Pacific-Ocean Internet
A Few Decades that Changed Society

The sea is dangerous and its storms terrible, but these obstacles have never been sufficient reason to remain ashore.
Ferdinand Magellan

The Web can be ascribed to one person, Tim Berners-Lee. Its conception, the first prototypes, the request for research funding, the drive to disseminate the Web as a documentation tool are all the merit of one man. On the contrary, the birth of the Internet cannot be rooted in the work of one single person, but rather of many dedicated individuals. Like an ocean receives water from many rivers and many storms, over the years and centuries, the Internet is what it is today thanks to many contributions, going from early theoretical work on packet-based networks, to practical efforts to create a prototype and make it work. The military-based project ARPANET is where these efforts came together in the first drop of the ocean to be, the Internet. What is astonishing is how something that started as a small research project could become so pervasive—flooding the whole world. Kay refers to this phenomenon as a natural resource, as the biggest of our oceans, the *Pacific*. Something peaceful that calmly connects continents and islands. Something shared and lively.

© Springer International Publishing AG, part of Springer Nature 2018
M. Aiello, *The Web Was Done by Amateurs*,
https://doi.org/10.1007/978-3-319-90008-7_2

2.1 ARPANET

The fact that the ARPANET was built to protect the United States in case of a Russian nuclear attack is a popular but false belief. It is correct that the origins of the ARPANET are tied to research financed by the US Government for defense purposes, but it had nothing to do with the specific case of a nuclear attack. One of the best accounts of the birth of the Internet was written to celebrate the first 25 years of its existence, organized by the American Defense Agency who originally commissioned it [58]. With all the confusion surrounding its origins and its relevance to the Web, it is necessary that we next consider the main milestones and reflect on why the Internet can be compared to something like the Pacific Ocean.

In the late 1950s, Russia's advancement was quite remarkable and the launch of the Sputnik was a universal announcement of their scientific and technological progress. One year later, in February 1958, the US president Dwight D. Eisenhower financed the foundation of the Advanced Research Projects Agency (ARPA), later to be known as Defense Advanced Research Project Agency (DARPA). Initially the agency had space exploration in its portfolio, which helped it attract a fair number of highly talented and motivated scientists and engineers. However, a few months later, with the transition of the 43-year-old National Advisory Committee for Aeronautics (NACA) into the National Aeronautics and Space Administration (NASA), the agency lost the responsibility for space and was devoted to basic research, focusing on high-risk, high-gain projects. This led to major changes in budget and a high turnover of directors. It was the third one, and the first scientist at the role, Jack Ruina, who brought a new academic style to the institution. He was not focusing on short-term results for the military. He liked a loose and open management style, being mostly interested in attracting top talents. Among the people that he had the merit of hiring was Joseph Carl Robnett Licklider, as the head of the Information Processing Techniques Office (IPTO). It was 1962 [117].

Licklider, better known as "Lick," was an American psychologist working at MIT, the same institution where Ruina was professor of electrical engineering. During his time at MIT, he was involved in the *Semi-Automatic Ground Environment (SAGE)* project, being responsible for the way radar data from multiple sites was presented to a human operator who had to make relevant military decisions.

In this way, Lick became acquainted with electronics and later with computing machinery, resulting in his understanding of their importance for society.

Lick's core idea was that of technology supporting the human being by carrying out work for him, beyond solving problems, but also being able to help the formulation of the problems in terms amenable to solution. The vision was elegantly presented in the famous paper MAN-COMPUTER SYMBIOSIS [80]. He does not see dominance of Artificial Intelligence over humans in the distant future, but rather a long period of men and computers working "in intimate association" and machines helping make complex decisions. According to Lick, the period of such association can run anywhere between 10 and 500 years or more, "but those years should be the most creative and exciting in the history of mankind."

Lick was a man of modesty, curiosity, and intuition; not only did he correctly predict the exciting times in which we live in today, but he also understood that computer resources had to be shared among more users. Using one computer for one person meant wasting resources given the clear time mismatch between human reasoning and speed of computation, that is, the computer waiting for human input when there is only one user. He also understood the potentials of computer-to-computer communication early on. In a 1963 ARPA memo, he uses the term "Intergalactic Network" in the headings, and he talks about the possibility of having "several different centers [...] netted together." Then he proceeds by elaborating on how these systems may exchange information and talk together. His focus is on interoperability at the level of distinct programming languages [81]. The following year, Lick left ARPA, but the computer networks seed had been sowed deeply in its soil. It was just a matter of time.

A few years later, ARPA set a budget for a "network experiment" strongly advocated by the new director of the IPTO department, Bob Taylor, someone who had come to admire the pioneering work of Licklider. By summer 1968, a request for quotes for *Interface Message Processors (IMP)*—that initial network experiment to involve four research sites—was sent out to 140 companies. It was a detailed document using terms such as "packets" of information and "store and forward." The terminology came from the work of Donald Watts Davis, a Welsh scientist working at the *British National Physical Laboratory (NPL)* who was convinced of the importance of breaking down information to be shared by computers into equally sized chunks. A similar idea was independently advocated by Paul Baran, an engineer working for the independent, military-oriented RAND research and consulting corporation, who called them "message blocks."

Some companies ignored the call, among them IBM, most likely because they considered it unfeasible to build such a network with small enough computer nodes at a reasonable price. In the end, the most convincing bid was made by a small Massachussets consulting firm: *Bolt Baranek and Newman (BBN)*. The firm's proposal was the most technologically sound and developed. One of the people behind the bid was Bob Kahn, who had left MIT in 1966 to join BBN. The small firm selected the Honeywell DDP-516 as the platform for their proposal, asking the manufacturer for some physical modifications to the basic machine. The foundation for their success in such a pioneering work lays in the ability to choose what to do in hardware and what in software, and to employ simple rules for error recovery (e.g., a lack of an acknowledgment for a packet is equivalent to asking for a new transmission of a packet). All this combined with the clever writing of compact code to perform the adaptive routing of packets and to enable the store and forward functionality.

The first two IMP machines were installed at the University of California at Los Angeles (UCLA) and at SRI, hosted by the group of Douglas Engelbart (Chap. 3). By the end of 1969, the universities of Utah and Santa Barbara were also connected (see Fig. 2.1). The first successful message on the ARPANET was transmitted from the UCLA computer via its IMP at 10:30 pm on October 29, 1969 to the SRI host. The two people attempting the transmission were also connected via a telephone line. UCLA sent the letter *l*, followed by *o* in the attempt to write the command "login." The transmission crashed when the third letter was sent from UCLA. Nevertheless, the first packages of the ARPANET were successfully sent; at that point, it was just a matter of debugging.

From there the network grew very rapidly. A few months later, the head-quarters of Bolt Baranek and Newman had been connected. One year later, 13 more nodes in the US were added (see Fig. 2.2). In 1973, the Norwegian Seismic Array connected to it, being the first non-American link. By 1981, the network rapidly grew to 213 nodes.

2.2 Comments, Please!

The driving spirit of collaboration that pervades the history of the Internet is beautifully captured by the way protocols and technologies have been discussed by the community since the early days. In the summer of 1968, graduate students from the four initial ARPANET sites met to discuss the emerging area of computer networking. They were keeping notes of their meetings and distributing them to members across the four sites. The notes were unassumingly called *Request for Comments (RFC)*. The first of these, "Host Software," discussed how to perform the initial "handshake" between

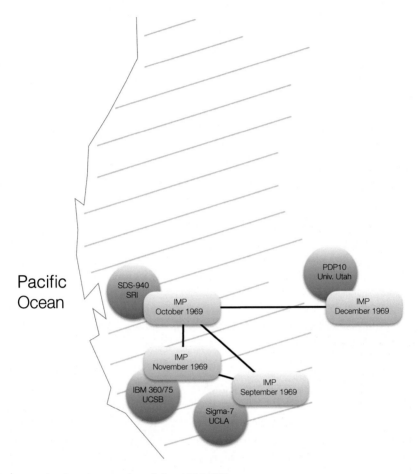

Fig. 2.1   The first four nodes of the ARPANET

two computers leading to the following interoperation between the machines. It was dated April 7, 1969.

Ever since, the RFC have first been the tool for protocol definition and discussion of the ARPANET and then official documents of the bodies governing the Internet, the *Internet Engineering Task Force (IETF)* and the *Internet Society (ISOC)*. As of today, RFCs can be of various kinds: *Informational, Experimental, Best Current Practice, Standards Track,* or *Historic.* RFC are the central documents that shape, and have shaped, the Internet and are on their way to reaching 10,000 instances [62]. Let's consider next a few historically fundamental ones for the development of the Internet.

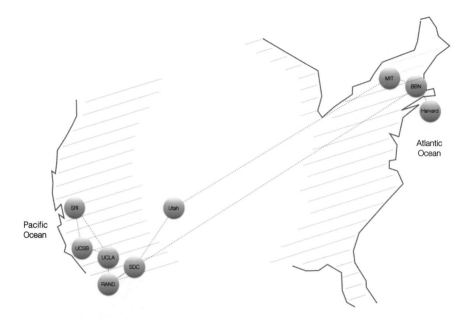

Fig. 2.2 The first additions to the ARPANET: MIT, Harvard, Utah, and the companies BBN, RAND, and SDC. Early 1970

RFC 114, April 1971.   The *File Transfer Protocol (FTP)* was the first application to showcase the ARPANET that did not involve a terminal-mainframe relation. Up to then, the network was designed to have terminals access the computational power remotely—the Telnet protocol (RFC 97) was an emblematic example. Due to Abhay Bhushan from MIT, FTP conceived a symmetric relation between the interacting hosts, where users authenticate and transfer textual or binary files. The protocol would travel over the *Network Control Program (NCP)*, the first transport protocol of the ARPANET (RFC 60). Since then, it has been updated a number of times before reaching its current form with improved security and the ability to travel over IPv6 (RFC 2428 and RFC 6384).

RFC 675, December 1974.   The *Specification of Internet Transmission Control Program (TCP)* is due to Bob Kahn and Vinton G. Cerf, who met during the first phase of installation of the IMP. Cerf was a graduate student at UCLA and interested in packet-based networks. He then went to Stanford with an assistant professor position, and was still involved in the ARPANET as chair of the IFIP working group TC6.1 on packet networks. He regularly met with Kahn who was interested in satellite packet networks and in radio-based ones.

They had long working sessions both on the East and West coast, trying to define a framework for the reliable transmission of messages via packet networks with a strong focus on hardware agnosticity. That is, satellite, radio, and IMP based networks should be able to "talk" to each other at the higher message transportation level. To achieve such interoperation, they proposed a new network element, the *Gateway*, what today would be called a router. Kahn put forward ideas to have network integration, no centralized control, and that lost packets would be detected and retransmitted [61]. This led to proposing the Transmission Control Program, which would later become the Transmission Control Protocol. The core ideas were published in a seminal paper in 1974 [34]. Soon after, the *Specification of Internet Transmission Control Program (TCP)* was distributed as RFC 675. The protocol defines the notion of a "connection" established between two nodes, possibly via a gateway. Information is broken into "internetwork packets" for the purpose of transmission. "In addition to acting like a postal service, the TCP insures end-to-end acknowledgment, error correction, duplicate detection, sequencing, and flow control."

RFC 760, January 1980.   The *DoD Standard Internet Protocol (IP)* RFC systematizes the previous ones on the Internet Protocol. It makes clear that it is about moving packets carrying sufficient routing information to reach their destination (called *datagrams*) and using hosts' addresses for the routing, independent of the message's content and purpose. By this time, the RFC had a unique editor, John Postel from UCLA. An early member of the ARPANET Community and friend of Cerf, Postel was using the very young network to "play" with SRI's NLS from UCLA. He retained the editorship of RFCs till his death, in 1998. RFC 760 is also famous for what is now known as Postel's Law: "an implementation should be conservative in its sending behavior, and liberal in its receiving behavior." The two protocols TCP and IP are often referred to in combination as the transport and internetworking layers, thus TCP/IP.

RFC 768, August 1980.   The *User Datagram Protocol (UDP)* RFC is just three pages long and, coherently, defines a simple datagram protocol. The idea is to have a simplified version of TCP not providing any ordering of packets, nor reliable delivering, thus requiring less overheads and complex network software to handle. Just five fields: source, destination, length, checksum, and data.

RFC 1149, April 1990.   The *Standard for the Transmission of IP Datagrams on Avia* defines the protocol for resorting to alternative physical means for the transportation of datagrams, specifically pigeons. Despite the high latency/low bandwidth, the protocol allows for having good collision avoidance mechanisms based on the pigeon's own visual system. Spring interactions among the pigeons can cause additional delays in that particular time of the year. This RFC was obviously released on April 1st as part of a tradition of humoristic yearly RFC documents released on April Fool's Day.

2.3   The Internet

By the end of the 1970s the ARPANET had grown to about 60 nodes, but only 10% of the United States' computer science departments were connected to it. As news about the network for sharing data and utilizing remote resources spread, the other academic institutions wanted to gain access to it. At the same time, having dedicated lines and hardware was expensive. Larry Landweber from University of Wisconsin coordinated an effort to obtain national funding for a computer science department network, with substantial help from Dorothy Robling Denning from Purdue University and Dave Farber from the University of Delaware. After some initial difficulties to get the grant approved, the operation was successful and the CSNET saw the light. It soon proved that a network like the ARPANET could also be built with less setup and management costs [58].

It was not the only new network. Inspired by the feasibility of something like the ARPANET, a number of new initiatives sprouted. The researchers in Magnetic Fusion Energy from the US Department of Energy realized the MFENet, while HEPNet was the network for the High Energy Physics researchers. The Space Physics Analysis Network (SPAN) became operational in December 1981 with three major nodes: University of Texas at Dallas, Utah State University, and Marshall Space Flight Center. It was not based on TCP/IP, but rather on Digital Equipment DCNET protocol [57].

In the early 1980s in Great Britain, there were various networks available at some universities that ran as independent projects. The people responsible for these started to discuss the possibility of interconnecting them. In April 1983, the Janet network went live, interconnecting about 50 sites by means of the X.25 protocol. One year later, Janet coordinators announced that the network ought to be available to the entire academic and scientific community, not just to computer science departments and researchers in the field. Soon thereafter, CSNET, the NSF-funded network that had evolved from the computer science departments' one was declared to be considered shared, "the connection must be made available to ALL qualified users on campus" [63].

Networks were thus transitioning from a specialized set of prototypes towards open utilities, paving the road to becoming natural resources.

It is in that period that the ARPANET shifted from the original NCP protocol (RFC 60) to the TCP/IP protocols (RFC 675 and RFC 760). That was January 1983, almost 10 years after its original proposal. The ARPANET was healthy and showing that it was robust beyond its prototype research status. However, it was expensive, costing DARPA $14 million a year to run, and had many new siblings around to take over its role [58]. By the end of 1989, DARPA decided to close the experimental network and have a celebrative symposium. The *Act One* symposium took place on August 17 and 18, 1989, at UCLA. Poems presented are the object of RFC 1121, authored by Postel, Kleinrock, Cerf, and Boehm.

2.4   Why Is It a Natural Resource?

The term Internet was first used by Cerf, Dalal, and Sunshine in 1974 in RFC 675, while introducing the foundations for TCP/IP-based networks. The idea was to add a layer of reliability and abstraction to support the interconnectivity of heterogenous networks. The design of the protocol was clean and effective, based on years of experience with the setting up of the initial ARPANET, and foresaw possible congestion problems. As often remarked by Leslie Lamport, a prominent scientist in the field of distributed systems, the issue with networks of computers is that the speed of sending data over links is orders of magnitude slower than that of the computation on a single machine. Therefore, there is a need for compensating the speed differences, buffering, queueing, and adjusting for data incoherences due to packages arriving in random order and clocks of different hosts not being synchronized. At a low datagram level, this is exactly what TCP/IP does. It anticipates that the network will run in varying conditions, that failures and omissions are the norm, and has several provisions for handling these situations.

For sure in 1974 it was hard to anticipate the size and scale the Internet was going to reach, though a good design took care of an ever-scaling infrastructure. If we consider the number of nodes, links, users, and traffic on the Internet today, it seems impossible that we are basically running on that same original design. The website Internet Live Stats offers an intriguing estimate of those values.[1] It suggests that today there are over 3.5 billion Internet users, over a billion websites, and 2 Exabytes of traffic in a day, that is, 10^{18} bytes. Interestingly, it also estimates the CO_2 emissions due to the Internet at over one million tons per day.

What is fascinating of the Internet is how naturally it scaled and still scales. In the foreword to a prominent TCP/IP handbook, Cerf acknowledges the unexpected growth. He states, "Reading through this book evokes a sense of wonder at the complexity that has evolved from a set of relatively simple concepts that worked with a small number of networks and application circumstances. As the chapters unfold, one can see the level of complexity that has evolved to accommodate an increasing number of requirements, dictated in part by new deployment conditions and challenges, to say nothing of sheer growth in the scale of the system" [47].

Predictions of the imminent failure of the Internet have cyclically appeared. Think of the initial skepticism around packet-based networks at AT&T in the early 1960s, or IBM not participating in the late 1960s' IMP tender due to its believed unfeasibility; then consider the doomsday scenarios portrayed when the Web started being successful.

A number of critics put forward that the transition from using the Internet for emails towards the Web, meaning the sending of "large" HTML files and images, would bring it to a grinding halt. In the mid-1990s, when Internet connectivity became a widespread home utility, the *last mile problem* was presented as insurmountable. The problem had to do with having to connect homes to the backbones of the Internet, thus covering the last mile of network distribution. The problem never really arose, as solutions rapidly appeared [108]. The success of new applications for the Internet, such as peer-to-peer (P2P) file sharing, Skype, and Voice over IP (VOIP), Bitorrent, and Video on Demand coincided with new reports of the imminent end of the Internet. Again, the alarmism was unjustified. Even very recently, the scale-free nature has been questioned—where scale-free is used to mean something that does not change its way of functioning depending on its size [53]. A way of measuring the quality of a design, is by considering how it stands the test of time. By this measure, the Internet and its TCP/IP foundation appear to have been an excellent design, something that can be compared to the road and aqueduct designs of the ancient Romans or—as Alan Kay does—to a natural resource such as the Pacific Ocean.

---

[1] www.internetlivestats.com.

A natural resource is something that, at least in principle, should be accessible to any human being and used by individuals who respect the rights and dignity of all others and of Nature. By this definition, the Pacific Ocean is surely a natural resource, and the discussion so far has brought enough arguments to support the Internet being one, too. This leads us to a new question, that is, what is a fair treatment of such a precious resource?

The TCP protocol has provisions to recover from package losses and packages arriving in random order, but it does not have any provisions for allowing one packet to intentionally pass one sent before. The original RFC 675 uses the word *priority* only once, and it is in the context of a bon ton rule rather than one of prevarication: "it appears better to treat incoming packets with higher priority than outgoing packets."[2]

Why would one need priorities and packages surpassing others anyway? The reason for advocating priorities is that it would allow better guarantees for some interactions, something usually referred to as a better Quality of Service (QoS). Applications requiring near real-time channels would have a higher likelihood of obtaining such resources with very low latencies and high throughput. However, allowing for priorities and intervening by authority on which packets to forward first introduces great risks. Some providers might intentionally delay or even omit packets of applications they do not favor. This is not just an hypothetical situation. This has happened in the past.

In 2004, Internet users in a rural area of North Carolina, who were connected via the service provider Madison River Communications, could not use Vonage's VoIP program, similar to the Skype application that uses the Internet as a phone carrier. The company had decided to block VoIP traffic to push its own telephone services, thus intervening on Internet packet forwarding, eventually dismissing those of the VoIP application. In 2008, Comcast was intervening on packets related to the peer-to-peer file sharing software Torrent by slowing them down and possibly omitting them [84]. In both cases, the Federal Communications Commission of the United States investigated and eventually posed an end to the practice.

As we have seen, the Internet works on the idea that applications send messages to each other. The messages are divided into packets of information that are put on the network and reach their intended destination. The packets rely on many machines, and many network links, to be taken care of, that is, stored and forwarded till they reach their intended destination. The practice of looking into the application related to the packet is known as *deep packet*

---

[2]The text is capitalized in the original RFC 675.

inspection, in contrast to the "shallow" approach of only storing and forwarding packets. Using information acquired in this way to decide on a policy for the forwarding of the package is considered a breach of *Net neutrality*.

The term Net neutrality was put forward in 2003 by Tim Wu, from Columbia University, who saw the risks of allowing fiddling with the fair package handling of the Web and pointed out the possible economic interest of the players in the telecommunication business for wanting to do so [124]. It is interesting to see that debate opinions can differ greatly. Most notably, the two main forces behind TCP/IP disagree. While Cerf is convinced that Net neutrality should be guaranteed to all, Kahn believes that not intervening on it will slow down technological innovation. Tim Berners-Lee is also a strong advocate of Net neutrality. Wu, in his 2003 defining paper, advocates an evolutionary approach to the Internet. He argues that one should not intervene on the Internet ecosystem, privileging one application over another, but rather let the fittest, most popular one emerge and flourish. Such vision supports the appropriateness of the Pacific-Ocean Internet metaphor.

3

Hypermedia Until the Web
From Microfilms to Electronic Links

I read a book cover to cover. It only took like two minutes, 'cause I went around the outside.
Demetri Martin

"You are Lone Wolf. In a devastating attack the Darklords have destroyed the monastery where you were learning the skills of the Kai Lords. You are the sole survivor." So started the book, FLIGHT FROM THE DARK, which I loved so much as a 12-year-old [43]. The book allowed me to make decisions about the story I was reading and define the script as I went along. For instance:

- "If you wish to defend the fallen prince, turn to 255."
- "If you wish to run into the forest, turn to 306."

It was possible to control, to some extent, the flow of the story and to help the prince, or die in the process. These kinds of "hypertextual" books were very popular in the 1980s. Their novelty resided in the breaking of the conventional reading order of a book. Readers did not traverse from the first to the final chapter, but rather read small text snippets, made a choice, and decided which page to jump to.

The idea was not entirely novel in literature. Writers had been experimenting with text fruition and trying to go beyond the traditional book format for several decades. Jorge Luis Borges, the Argentinian author, has been credited with being at the forefront of such a movement, and often people see in his 1941 short story THE GARDEN OF FORKING PATHS the first example of an

© Springer International Publishing AG, part of Springer Nature 2018
M. Aiello, *The Web Was Done by Amateurs*,
https://doi.org/10.1007/978-3-319-90008-7_3

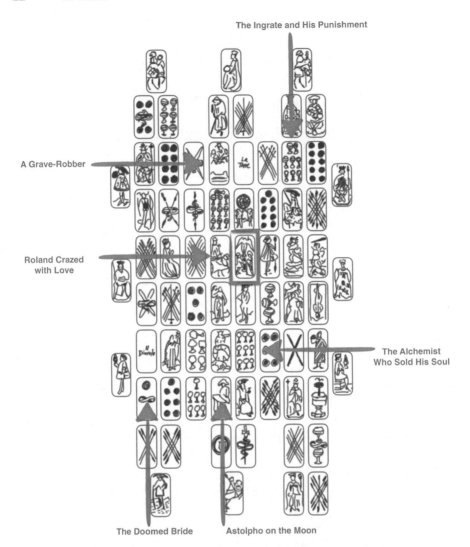

Fig. 3.1 Some of the stories in The Castle of Crossed Destinies

hypertextual story [23]. This is partially true, or better said, it is true at the meta-level. In fact, the text of the story is read without breaking the sequential order, though the story describes the possibility of having infinitely many story developments happening concurrently. Just imagine that you are at a given moment of time and branching from there are potentially infinite futures, and you take all of them at the same time [111].

An exploration of the combinatorics of story creation is the driving force behind Italo Calvino's THE CASTLE OF CROSSED DESTINIES [30]. The Italian novelist embarked on a project to add short stories to a recently discovered deck of tarocks dating back to the fifteenth century and commissioned by the noble Visconti family. Set in a remote magic castle where the guests lose their voices, an unacquainted set of people meet. Each one of them "tells" his story, using tarock cards rather than words. The cards are laid on a table and, depending on the direction one reads them, they tell different stories. Calvino was convinced that the cards could provide a huge amount of stories in almost any of their random combinations. The text of the book is not hypertextual in a modern sense, though one has the impression that the order in which the chapters are read does not really matter. It is the two-dimensional spatial pattern the cards form on the table that does.

The relation of the layout of the cards to the formation of stories or chapters is shown in Fig. 3.1. Take for instance the Love card, highlighted with a red box in the center of Fig. 3.1. The card is part of the story of Roland (read from left to right on the tarock grid). It indicates the Love angel revealing to Roland that his precious one, Angelica, was falling in love with someone else: the young "Jack of Woods," indicated by the card on the right of the Love angel. The same card is used in the story of Astolpho, who goes to the moon to try to recover Roland's sanity (read from bottom to top in the tarock grid). In this story, the Love card represents the concept of Eros, "pagan god, that the more one represses, the more is devastating," and the ultimate reason for Astolpho's going to the moon [30]. Stories are thus created by the combination of laying cards on a surface, while the same card supports more stories based on its context and overall reading order.

$$\sim$$

What is hypertext? Modern definitions refer to the reading order. Traditional text is purely sequential. In the Western cultures, one starts at the top-left and proceeds left to right, top to bottom. Once a page is finished, one turns that page to the left and continues with the same rule of reading, and so on left to right till there are no more pages left—something that makes automation of reading amenable to mechanization [3]. Hypertextuality breaks these kinds of sequential rules. In the text, there can be references, called *hyperreferences*, that allow the reader to make a choice and proceed either sequentially or to jump to another set of words somewhere else in the same document set.

A simple and effective way of modeling this is by using graphs. One can think of words or text snippets as nodes and the possibility of jumping as edges in the graph. The graph that one obtains defines the type of hypertextuality of the document. A traditional book becomes what is known in graph theory as a *chain*—Chapter 1 linked to Chapter 2, linked to Chapter 3, and so on. This book being an example. One might argue that there is already some weak form of hypertextuality even here: while reading a chapter, one jumps to the reference section, following the number, and then comes back to the main text; or one follows a footnote pointer, to resume sequential reading thereafter. If we were to account for this, one could say that the book is a very unbalanced *binary tree*. Adventure stories like the FLIGHT FROM THE DARK are best described as *directed acyclic graphs (DAG)s*, as one navigates from the first chapter towards any of the many final ones by following many possible routes.[1] Some of these books are not entirely cycle free, though, as it is possible to come more than once to the same chapter (examples are the loops 140-36-323-290-140, 130-201-130, and 238-42-147-238 in Joe Dever's FLIGHT FROM THE DARK), though these are exceptions to the dominant DAG structure. It is also typical to have only one source node and several sink nodes, meaning that the book has one start but many possible endings. Michael Niggel's visual analysis of the paths and endings of Raymond Almiran Montgomery's JOURNEY UNDER THE SEA is also a nice example of "choose your own story" textual organizations.[2] The book is a DAG and there are 42 possible endings to the story, most of them unfavourable to the reader. That's life.

Finally, there is the most free form of hypertextuality, the one with no constraints over the edges and nodes. Links can go from any given piece of text to any other one. This is simply a *generic graph*. The best example is certainly the Web. When modeling web pages as nodes and hypertextual references as links, as is typical, we obtain a graph that embeds chains, binary trees, and cycles. The Web is the collective effort of a myriad of uncoordinated people, so there is little structure to it, one might think. On the other hand, the collective effort takes, as we will see in greater detail in Chap. 9, the form of a *scale-free network*. Figure 3.2 depicts the most typical forms of (hyper)-textuality.

The world of literature was not the only one questioning the sequential flow of storytelling and information fruition. In the scientific and technological world, a number of proposals and systems have been launched in the past century. These go beyond text as the sole form of conveying information, and are about media, more broadly speaking. While the word hypertext has been around for a while, the term *hypermedia* appears soon after the birth of the Web, most likely due to Ted Nelson. He used it to refer to the non-sequential fruition of text, images, videos, and basically any other form of representation

---

[1] Figure 1 is also an example of a DAG.

[2] See the visualization at https://flowingdata.com/2009/08/11/choose-your-own-adventure-most-likely-youll-die/.

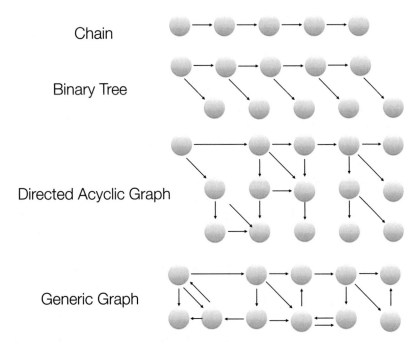

Fig. 3.2 Types of (hyper)-textuality

of information. In fact, what might be the very first form of hypermedia was based on microfilms, the high-density storage media of the middle of the last century.

3.1 How We May Think

Coming from a family of whaling captains, Vannevar Bush knew that one must attack things frontally and pro-actively, as he reflected on his ancestors having "a way of running things with no doubt." An essential quality when governing a ship and managing a crew. And indeed, Bush ran many shows. Educated at Tufts and MIT, he decided to get a PhD in one year, and managed to do so in 1916. He went on combining academic achievements and entrepreneurial successes. Refining the idea behind a patent for making radio receiving apparatuses, he co-founded the American Appliances Company in 1922, which later became an electronics giant, Raython. He worked on a machine to mechanize first-order differential equations. He was appointed Dean of Engineering at MIT and vice president in 1932. While World War II unfolded, Bush was a central figure in determining the scientific agenda of the United States. He had directorship roles with the Carnegie Institute of Washington, National Advisory Committee for Aeronautics (later to become NASA), and acted as the main scientific advisor of President Franklin Delano Roosevelt. His proposal for a National Research Committee was approved in 1940 by the president on the spot on the basis of a one-page proposal. Bush had a modern approach to research management where delegation and trust had major roles. Whenever a proposal for a research project was presented, he simply asked, "Will it help to win a war; this war?" Showing his openness to any suggestion and his goal-driven approach.

One of his major achievements was supporting the communication between the scientists and the military. This was particularly true for a crucial secret effort he helped established and foster: the Manhattan Project. The project eventually led to the first nuclear bomb, and the consequent ending of World War II [64].

Exposed to so many research efforts and results, Bush was reflecting on the human way of reasoning and on the possible ways to support it. He was convinced that the human associative memory could be supported, while the human body of knowledge was growing very rapidly. He felt the threat of specialization and growing amounts of information, and he pondered how to manage these modern challenges. The idea of a machine to address these issues had already emerged in his thoughts in the 1930s. The *Memex* became a concrete proposal in the famous 1945 article As WE MAY THINK [29].

In the article, Bush envisions a future of intelligent machines, of head-mounted cameras to capture what a user sees, and of desk machines to provide information and association ability to their users. That's right, 70 years ago, Bush had already imagined an "information technology" desk on which to browse information and follow links. The magnetic-coated and silicon-based materials of the modern desktop were not available. Instead, Bush envisioned using the best storage technology of the time: microfilm. The ability to associate and move from one set of data to another one was enabled by the mechanical operation of several tapes of microfilms. Some microfilms could be "written" on the spot by the machine itself. This was the Memex.

Memex was never built as a prototype, but a quite accurate design was provided by Bush in the article (see Fig. 3.3). An effective animation showing how the Memex would work was presented during the 1995 ACM SIGIR conference, and it is available on-line.[3] The desk has two screens for viewing information, such as book pages, and one acquisition camera (something like a

---

[3]YouTube video: https://youtu.be/c539cK58ees.

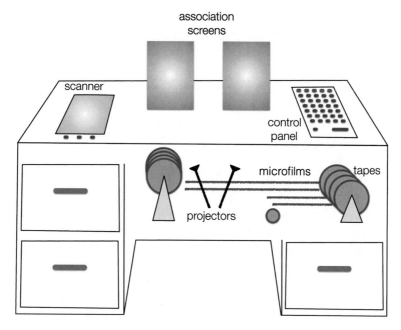

Fig. 3.3 The envisioned Memex, inspired by Bush's original sketch [29]

modern scanner) to acquire new information. A set of control buttons drive the mechanical control of the various microfilm tapes and are visible on the top left of the desk. The user is able to associate information viewed on the screens—that is, create links between the microfilms—and to add personal notes to them. By simply providing a keyword or symbol to Memex, a "trail of facts" is followed to provide the key associated and personalized information. The trail of facts is effectively a set of relations among the keywords and symbols.

Bush's intuition and vision are impressive. What he designed is an hypermedia personal repository, something that in terms of information organization is very similar to a personal, one desktop Web. Furthermore, he talks about thinking machines and augmenting the human capabilities. Today, we are used to hearing the term Artificial Intelligence (AI), and we credit John McCarthy for formally opening this as a field of science during the 1956 Dartmouth workshop. The work of Alan Turing on machine intelligence in the early 1950s is indicated as the seminal sprout for the birth of AI. But the vision of Bush is antecedent even to all these fundamental contributions! Bush might have missed the potentials of computing and digitalization, but he surely understood the power of information and its relevance for augmenting the human cognitive capabilities.

Quite juicy for a scientist, Bush also notes in AS WE MAY THINK that "Publication has been extended far beyond our present ability to make use of the record." One does wonder what he would think of today's world where there is a journal dedicated to almost any scientific endeavor and some scientists have the ability—and feel the urge—to publish over 100 papers per year. Yes, there are some stakhanovists among us who write a paper every 3 days, including weekends [2].

3.2   The oN-Line System (NLS)

The work of Bush is appreciated and is still modern after 70 years. It actually has been influential from the very beginning. In particular, a scientist of the Stanford Research Institute (today simply called SRI), Douglas Engelbart, was very motivated by it. Engelbart read Bush's AS WE MAY THINK while in the army just after World War II and decided early in his life that he wanted to make the world a better place, rather than just settle on a steady job with a fixed pay. Having this in mind, he looked for positions that would allow him to support humanity and saw in the digital computer the means for achieving that. He then got a master's degree, a PhD, and started an academic position at UC Berkeley. However, he felt that he could not realize his dream inside academia and left. He later joined SRI in Menlo Park. His 1962 paper AUGMENTING HUMAN INTELLECT: A CONCEPTUAL FRAMEWORK sets the foundations of his vision [46]. He considered the tasks humans were presented with to be growing exponentially in complexity, and therefore humans needed appropriate tools to augment their capabilities. This augmentation went in the direction of Memex, having information linked together and available at ones fingertips.

Unlike with today's iPads and tablets, technology at your fingertips had quite a different meaning in the 1960s. Back then, simply having multiple users interacting concurrently with a computer was a challenge, and the interfaces were sequences of characters on a terminal, or paper cards and tapes to punch. Engelbart came up with an ingenious patent. A wooden box with two perpendicular wheels that could sense the motion of the box on a surface. The box was wired, having thus a cable coming out one of the shorter ends of the box, and giving it a friendly animal shape, that of a mouse. A patent awarded in 1970 defined the birth of what is the major computer interaction device to date, the computer mouse, which in Engelbart's plans was the input device to interact graphically on a two dimensional grid with a computer. In fact, one of Engelbart's innovations was the proposal of integrating keyboard-based input, with a mouse to be used with the right hand, and five special keys for the left hand.

The oN-Line System (NLS) was developed by a team led by Engelbart in the early 1960s and was demoed at the end of 1968 at the San Francisco Fall Joint Computer Conference. The demo was epic. Engelbart set up a dedicated video link to the labs in Menlo Park, 50 km further south, and used a giant projector borrowed from NASA. The demo has since been known as the *Mother of All Demos*, something that truly showed the power of hyperlinked media, videoconferencing, and the use of a mouse to move on a screen filled with text. That was 1968.

In terms of hypertext, NLS was the first system to actually be built. The hypertextuality was perhaps a bit naïve compared to today's systems, but it was surely supported. The idea is that text segments get unique identifiers that are assigned according to their location in hierarchically structured files. One can also assign other identifiers, which are ordered following the time at which they were created. It is possible to refer to those text identifiers and to "follow" them as links. The mouse has a central role in enabling the clicking on the link identifier, though it is also possible to follow a link by typing its identifier directly. The system allows the user to jump back to a link source. Scripts also existed in NLS that allowed the creation of links, that is, when clicking on a specific word, the system could try to find a description in a specific glossary file, therefore allowing one to effectively follow a just-in-time created hyperlink.

3.3 Xanadu

Another American innovator, Ted Nelson, was deeply influenced by Bush's vision. Having a background in philosophy and sociology, he was interested in the role of relations among concepts in knowledge. He introduced novel terms to represent various declinations of such relations: *hypertext, transclusions, intertwingularity, zippered lists,* and *ZigZag*. He was convinced that the sequential nature of text organization is deeply unnatural and cannot capture human knowledge well enough. He often referred to such sequential text organization—with a derogatory connotation—as "paper."

Such discontent led him to start, in 1960, a mastodontic project on building a computer-based system for the storage, retrieval, and interaction with text. Named after the city of residence of the Mongol ruler in Samuel Taylor Coleridge's poem A VISION IN A DREAM: A FRAGMENT, the Xanadu project

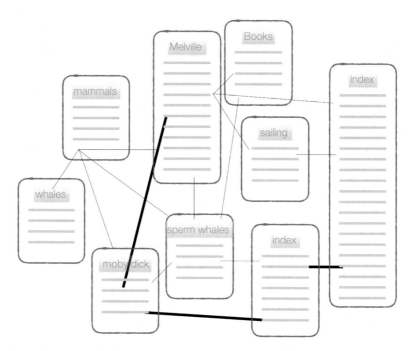

Fig. 3.4 Hypertextual document relations in Xanadu, showing links and transclusions

has been running for over 50 years. In Xanadu, documents are compositions of text fragments as expressed by a set of bidirectional links. A document has several versions that can be compared, and its evolution can be traced while comparing the changes between versions. Users are uniquely identified, and copyright is traceable via permanent links. The bidirectionality of links guarantees accountability and avoids dangling references. Forms of micro-payments to honor royalties can be implemented to provide support for authorship and content syndication.

Nelson's 1965 paper about file structure, the one where the term *hypertext* was coined, has examples of list structures and what a Xanadu document would look like [91]. As an example, Nelson shows hyper-linked text as an historian, interested in writing a book, could assemble and integrate in Xanadu. Figure 3.4 shows the network structure among documents with two types of relationships. The thin lines represent links, while the thick lines represent *transclusions*, that is, inclusions of parts of a document into another one. Transclusion is a term that Nelson introduced later, though the concept can already be found in the original 1965 paper [92].

Nelson, a strong character who loves to be controversial and direct, considers "cut and paste" a sin of modern computer technology. Text should not be cut, but bidirectionally linked. The text is alive and changing, so versioning must be supported. The current Xanadu's official website lists the core requirements and makes a point of showing that current systems, including the Web, only satisfy a few of these. Each requirement is very interesting and worth a reflection in its own right. Using the enumeration of the Xanadu project website, these are the requirements:

2a   Every Xanadu server is uniquely and securely identified.

2b   Every Xanadu server can be operated independently or in a network.

2c   Every user is uniquely and securely identified.

2d   Every user can search, retrieve, create, and store documents.

2e   Every document can consist of any number of parts, each of which may be of any data type.

2f   Every document can contain links of any type, including virtual copies (transclusions), to any other document in the system accessible to its owner.

2g   Links are visible and can be followed from all endpoints.

2h   Permission to link to a document is explicitly granted by the act of publication.

2i   Every document can contain a royalty mechanism at any desired degree of granularity to ensure payment on any portion accessed, including virtual copies (transclusions) of all or part of the document.

2j   Every document is uniquely and securely identified.

2k   Every document can have secure access controls.

2l   Every document can be rapidly searched, stored, and retrieved without user knowledge of where it is physically stored.

2m   Every document is automatically moved to physical storage appropriate to its frequency of access from any given location.

2n   Every document is automatically stored redundantly to maintain availability even in case of a disaster.

2o   Every Xanadu service provider can charge their users at any rate they choose for the storage, retrieval, and publishing of documents.

2p Every transaction is secure and auditable only by the parties to that transaction.

2q The Xanadu client–server communication protocol is an openly published standard. Third-party software development and integration is encouraged.

Xanadu puts a great emphasis on unique identification of content and authors, and on bidirectional links that avoid the problem of dangling pointers. It also pushes the notion of networked information and having several repositories. The focus is on the data structure and organization, rather than the user experience per se, which was more central to Engelbart's heart. Ted Nelson has always been very critical to the Web, while calling Engelbart a friend. Nelson refers to Engelbart as having a similar ambition as his own: "We have different agenda's, but we have very much the same attitude towards how things are" [93].

The work of Ted Nelson, perhaps encouraged by his strong and poignant personality, has been often criticized. In a famous article that appeared in *Wired* magazine, Xanadu is defined as "the longest-running vaporware project in the history of computing—a 30-year saga of rabid prototyping and heart-slashing despair." Others have called Nelson "one of the most influential contrarians in the history of the information age" [45, 121]. While it is true that today's world does not run on Xanadu, and the early prototypes never had a chance of becoming real products, one must say that the design principles and visions of Xanadu are sound and would have been greatly beneficial to today's Web, had they been taken into account. Kay is critical of the computational nature of the Web; Nelson of the data and relationship organization. Two very valid points against the design of one of the largest information systems to date.

3.4   HyperCard

After NLS and Xanadu, designs, tools, and technologies having some form of hypertextuality and hypermediality started to appear. A seasoned, but definitely still very valid account in many of the technological efforts in that direction, is offered in a 1987 paper by Jeff Conklin [41]. If most of the systems listed in Conklin's paper are concerned with the fruition of text, few put the emphasis on the computational aspect. A prominent example is HyperCard, released by Apple in 1987. HyperCard comes from the innovative talent of Bill Atkinson, one of the first Apple employees and the mind behind the graphics packages of the first Macintosh and MacPaint application. Atkinson wanted to build a system that would allow simple organization of information in the form of cards, something like a nice graphical database. He also teamed up with the HyperTalk programming language team at Apple to provide scripting ability within its cards. With HyperCard, one could put text, images, and other files inside a card and then add buttons with behaviors. The typical behavior was that of jumping to another card, but one could also have more elaborate scripts, including the calling of external applications. HyperCard was a huge success, as it brought to a number of non-programmers a tool that they could easily program. The ability to have buttons with simple programmable behaviors and to visually see the objects as cards of a same collection was intuitive and effective.

HyperCard differs from most hypertextual systems, as its links are typically not associated with words or terms, but rather with actions. Buttons, scripts, and events can make the user jump from one card to another. In that sense, it resembles an hypermedia rather than an hypertextual system. Furthermore, the network does not have a prominent role in HyperCard. It is more a database of object states; each card is stored in permanent memory as a file of its contents, scripts, and values of the stored objects.

Interestingly, Jeff Conklin's own paper on the hypertextual systems was initially released as an HyperCard file and later translated into the paper format by Paolo Petta [41].

3.5 Enquire and the Birth of the Web

Unlike the previous inventors and researchers who had a vision to change the world, the Web sprung out of a hobby project of a brilliant physicist. Tim Berners-Lee is the child of two mathematicians who participated in the first British production of a computer, the `Ferranti Mark 1`. He earned a bachelor's in physics from the prestigious Queen's College at Oxford. He then picked up a job in telecommunications and yet another one developing printing software, both in the Southwest of England. In 1980, he took a six-months job as a contractor at CERN, the European Organization for Nuclear Research, globally known for operating the largest particle physics laboratory in the world. His task was to contribute to a new control system for two of its particle accelerators, whose development was lagging behind. This event proved to be life-changing for him and, later, for the world.

Back then there was little of a computer network at CERN. Actually, many scientists did not even have a personal terminal in their office. Still, the experiments were producing a large amount of data. Berners-Lee was both intrigued and mesmerized by the research center, its facilities, and its people, while being frustrated by the hurdles that made it difficult to access data and foster collaboration. For a newcomer to the center, just understanding who was who and working on which project was a nightmare.

He decided to build a system for his own personal use, while working on the control system software. He recalls, "I wrote it in my spare time and for my personal use, and for no loftier reason than to help me remember the connections among the various people, computers, and projects at the lab" [19]. It was the birth of `Enquire`. The software was named after a 1856 book on do-it-yourself, bon ton advice, ENQUIRE UPON EVERYTHING, which has seen more than 125 editions to date [98]. The core idea of Enquire is that information is organized in nodes and links. Nodes represent people, projects, and data items in general. They are like cards with information and links. A new node can be made only by creating a link from an old node, thus avoiding islands of information. Links are of two types: internal to a document and then bidirectional, or external, and then unidirectional. Links also have a simple form of annotation, illustrating the relation represented by the link. Originally these relations were: *made, includes, uses, describes* and their inverses *was made by, is part of, is used by, described by.* A very basic semantic annotation to explain why two nodes are related. Note that this is far from the Semantic Web concept that was advocated by the same Berners-Lee 20 years later. The Semantic Web is the focus of Chap. 8.

There was no explicit description of an ontology of concepts, e.g., saying that Tim is a physicist and that the concept of a physicist is included in the concept of a scientist was not represented and could not bring Enquire to conclude that Tim is a scientist. Interestingly, the system had bidirectional links, unlike the modern Web. The system was centralized, being a monolithic application with its own database. Well, it was simply a system built by Berners-Lee on the development machine for his own use. The system did not have random access to its data or an advanced query facility, the intention being the "surfing" of the link structure: beginning from the start page and following the links till one hits the information sought.

Less than four years later, Berners-Lee returned to CERN on a permanent contract. Now more computers and terminals were available. That was the same year the first Apple Macintosh was introduced to the market, and the idea of personal computers was becoming more widely accepted. In 1985, there was a person responsible for TCP/IP implementation, and the protocol of the Internet was starting to be used internally. It was not until January 1989 that CERN would be connected to the ARPANET (Chap. 2) as the first European institutions were joining the American network, having the Dutch research institute for mathematics and computer science (CWI) as the entry point [104]. While working at CERN, Tim Berners-Lee resumed work on Enquire and was encouraged to seek internal funding for its further development.

In March 1989, Tim Berners-Lee internally submitted INFORMATION MANAGEMENT: A PROPOSAL for funding. Motivated by the amount of information available at CERN and the difficulty of managing and retrieving it, he argued that "a 'web' of notes with links (like references) between them is far more useful than a fixed hierarchical system." Berners-Lee then referred explicitly to HyperText, quoting Ted Nelson, and to the first conference and special journal issue on the topic. In the proposal, he also mentioned HyperCard as a related system, though criticized the lack of distribution in it: "A difference was that Enquire, although lacking the fancy graphics, ran on a multiuser system, and allowed many people to access the same data." This is surely correct. However, one could argue that the object-oriented design and the ability to run scripts and code within the system were essential features that Enquire could have incorporated.

Tim Berners-Lee, among other things, mentioned the possibility of using Enquire for performing automatic data analysis. He writes, "An intriguing possibility, given a large hypertext database with typed links, is that it allows some degree of automatic analysis. It is possible to search, for example, for anomalies such as undocumented software or divisions which contain no people." This is an incredibly visionary statement. The Web is a "large database" today, actually it is a huge one. Indeed, it is possible to analyze data and draw conclusions from it. One could argue that such data analytics is *the core business* of companies like Google, Facebook, and Amazon. The size and freshness of the information available on the Web has potentially infinite uses for classification and prediction purposes—for instance, to forecast the timing and size of flu spreading [1, 76].

The proposal was marked as "Vague but exciting" by the team leader, Mike Sendall, and got approved [123]. It also contained a diagram providing an example regarding information systems at CERN, including all core components of the proposed Enquire system. A diagram inspired by the one in the proposal, but about novels and authors, is shown in Fig. 3.5. Concepts are cloud shapes, documents are trapezoidal, links are arrows with annotation as text, and ovals represent instances. Some of the entities are hierarchically organized.

Having had the proposal accepted, Tim Berners-Lee needed to build the system and seek support for it outside CERN, too. In 1990, hypertext was

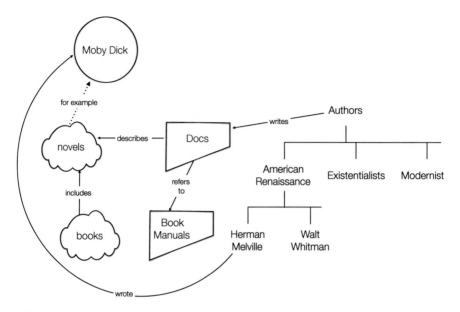

Fig. 3.5 Diagram inspired by the one in the original 1989 proposal of Tim Berners-Lee for the Web

a "hot" research topic. There had already been two ACM international conferences on hypertext organized, one in 1987 at Chapel Hill and another in 1989 in Pittsburgh. The first edition of the European conference on the topic was organized in 1990 in France. Tim Berners-Lee attended the latter and saw some interesting prototypes. Unfortunately, he did not receive the support he was hoping for.

Back at CERN, he decided to prototype the system himself. He managed to get a just-released NeXT machine (a very powerful personal computer coming from the vision of Steve Jobs who, at the time, was no longer with Apple), and in October 1990 he started developing the protocols and technology for Enquire in Objective-C, the core programming language of the NeXT. By mid-November of that year, he had a graphical browser which he called WorldWideWeb, and by December he had defined a markup language for the representation of hypertextual documents, HTML. The browser could, in addition to displaying HTML content, also be used as an editor for the same. Finally, a fast protocol to retrieve HTML documents was designed, the HyperText Transfer Protocol (HTTP), which rapidly proved to outperform the more established File Transfer Protocol (FTP). The final ingredient was a *universal* way to retrieve the content, as there was no central repository on the Web. This took the form of what now are known as Universal Resource

Identifiers (URIs). In those few months, Tim Berners-Lee put together the three core components of the Web: HTML , HTTP, and URIs. The rest is just software to showcase and demonstrate them.

The first 10 years of the Web are presented first-hand in Tim Berners-Lee's own book [19]. In short, the initial years were dedicated to developing prototypes and finding people interested in participating in the system. Early adopters included the *Stanford Linear Accelerator Center (SLAC)* whose director saw the potential of the system for organizing their own data, and some enthusiasts who went on to develop clients and servers for the platform of their choice using the programming language they fancied the most. During that phase, Tim Berners-Lee understood the importance of standardization, interoperation, and keeping the platform open and available. He insisted that CERN release everything related to the Web as open source, and the request was granted in 1994. Next, he pursued the standardization of the URIs. The original proposal was to call such naming schema Universal Document Identifiers, but IETF members were opposed to the terms, especially "Universal." Berners-Lee gave up on the name, preferring to make sure that URIs were standardized and preferring to make sure that browsers, and more generally systems, were built that could access resources via several protocols, e.g., HTTP and FTP.

The Web saw an incredibly rapid and vast spreading. Tim Berners-Lee has honorably put most of his focus on keeping it an open platform. Standardization and openness have been his driving goal, despite the huge economic interests that have since arisen around the technology. Towards the end of 1994, Tim Berners-Lee founded the *World Wide Web Consortium (W3C)*, originally hosted at MIT with support from the European Commission and DARPA. W3C has since been very vigilant concerning any attempt to start dialects of any protocols, especially those dictated by commercial interests. W3C promotes a set of core principles and components that must be in all implementations of their protocols.

∼

By his own admission, when Enquire saw its birth, Tim Berners-Lee was not acquainted with the work of Bush, Nelson, and Engelbart [19]. He says that he saw the video about the "Mother of All Demos" only in 1994. He talks about discussing the idea of representing data as circles and links with his colleagues at CERN. The merits of Tim Berners-Lee are evident. He made a system that worked well, he stood behind it with modesty and perseverance, and he did not "sell" it, but instead went for global accessibility and welfare. This spirit and such intentions are admirable and knightship worthy. In the BBC interview following his 2004 Knight nomination, he states that his knightship "proves what can happen to ordinary people who work on things that happen to work out, like the Web" [15]. In a following interview, he modestly states to have just been "in the right place at the right time" [16].

At the same time, the history of hypermedia and of the Web provides plenty of clues to understand Alan Kay's 2012 statement. If being an amateur implies not being acquainted with the history of a field and not mastering the state of the art, then Kay is surely right. Tim Berners-Lee designed a system ignoring most of the previous work on hypertextuality. He also seemed unfamiliar with the innovation in databases and data representation. The decade before Enquire had seen many interesting proposals. The idea of having databases organized in relational forms, a major disruption to the rather sequential organization used up until then, was promoted by the IBM researcher Edgar Codd who published a fundamental paper in 1970 [39]. A few years later, Peter Pin-Shan Chen proposed a model for representing data made of entities and relationships among them. In the 1975 paper WHAT'S IN A LINK: FOUNDATIONS FOR SEMANTIC NETWORKS, William Wood proposes a linked data structure to describe concepts useful for representing knowledge [122]. All these efforts appear to have been outside the radar of Berners-Lee when he worked on Enquire and later proposed the Web.

Such facts fuel the impression that there is a great amount of reinventing the wheel in the birth of the Web. Not plagiarism or malicious utilization of other people's ideas, but simply a lack of the background for designing a system that would become so widespread and central to humankind. Can this explain the remark of Kay that the Web was done by amateurs?

Part II

The Web

4

The Original Web Pattern
URL, HTTP, and HTML

*The most important thing that was new was the idea of URI or URL, that any
piece of information anywhere should have an identifier, which will allow you to
get hold of it.*
Tim Berners-Lee

During the birth and evolution first of the Internet and then the Web, the
computer world was going through major transformations. Beginning with
expensive machines available to few institutions and companies, shared by
many individuals, the world was rapidly moving towards computers which
were privately affordable and thus becoming personal. Slowly, electronic computation left the work environments to become part of our home furniture.
A few visionaries saw this coming. Alan Kay in his PhD thesis, defended
in 1969 at the University of Utah, and later in his 1972 paper illustrates a
futuristic device called the DynaBook. This device appears to have all the
features that we are used to in a modern laptop [68]. About 15 years later,
Mark Weiser, a creative scientist working at Xerox PARC, envisioned a world
of internetworked devices of all sizes, from interactive walls to portable pads.
He called this way of computing *ubiquitous*, effectively opening a new area of
research and development for computer scientists [119].

In the early 1960s, one of the most popular computers of the time, the
PDP-1, would sell for about $120,000, comparable to a million dollars today.
Back then, being a popular computer meant that a few dozen were sold: 53
to be precise [40]. Owning such an expensive infrastructure meant that it was
best utilized by sharing among many employees. The sharing was obtained by

© Springer International Publishing AG, part of Springer Nature 2018
M. Aiello, *The Web Was Done by Amateurs*,
https://doi.org/10.1007/978-3-319-90008-7_4

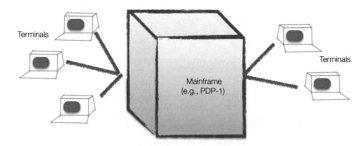

Mainframe and Terminals, late 1950s/early 1960s

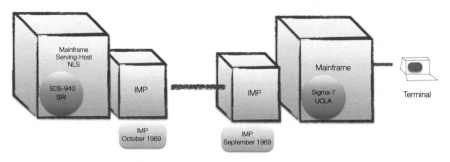

Serving-host in the early ARPANET, late 1960s

Fig. 4.1 Towards client-server architectures

having a number of terminals directly connected to the machine. These were basic screens and keyboards that could interactively issue commands to the main central computer (top of Fig. 4.1).

The experimentation of the ARPANET and other first private networks created the possibility to use a terminal in one laboratory to execute tasks on a computer in another lab. Remember Postel playing with NLS at SRI from UCLA (Sect. 2.2)? In this case, the SRI computer was considered to be the *serving-host*, terminology first appearing in the 1969 RFC 4. Bottom of Fig. 4.1 illustrates this example using the labels of the map from Fig. 2.1. In the 1970s, the term *client-server* was commonly used at Xerox PARC to describe a computer performing computation requested by another computer or terminal via a network link. The architecture became the standard with the emergence of computer networks and naturally became the one central to the Web. In the client-server architecture, the client has the software to locate Web resources (that is, pages identified by URLs) and it can render them, subsequently following links in them. The Web server has a number of pages in its possession.

The next natural step in the evolution of distributed architectures has been the separation between the repository of pages, e.g., using a database, and the software responsible for interacting with the client, the Web server. This led to the so-called *three-tier architecture*. The concept has since been generalized into n-tier or multi-tier architectures, where the service of pages can be modularized in several components, typically separating the application logic from the data repository, as shown in Fig. 4.2.

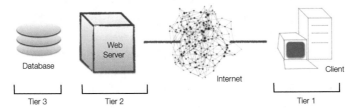

The Client-server Web interaction, late 1980s

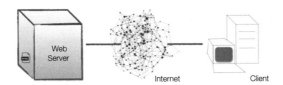

The three-tier Web architecture, mid-1990s

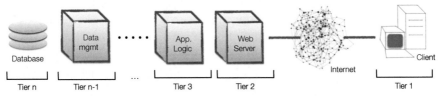

The n-tier Web architecture, late 1990s

Fig. 4.2 The evolution of client-server architectures

The core idea of the Web is quite simple and based on three core technologies/protocols. First, the object at the basis of the Web is an hypertextual document. That is, text with links to other documents. To describe these documents, Tim Berners-Lee defined the *HyperText Markup Language* (HTML). These documents can reside on any machine without centralized indices or control. To access the document, he defined a file exchange protocol, named *HyperText Transfer Protocol (HTTP)*. The protocol uses the TCP/IP suite by working at the application level. Finally, there must be a way of finding such documents despite the lack of a centralized index system. The addressing of Web resources is achieved via *Uniform Resource Locators (URL)s*. These combine pieces of information about the machine hosting the page to be found with some machine-dependent addressing for the specific resource, typically, a file system descriptor. That's it. The Web is simply based on these three technologies defining a clear interaction pattern:

> repeat: find a resource using a URL, interact with HTTP, obtain HTML documents, and display them to the user.

Browsing HTML documents means following new URLs, and the pattern repeats itself indefinitely.

The display should consider that text is mixed with hyperlinks that can refer to other pages anywhere in the text. In other words, the initial Web was a distributed file system, without any centralized control, openly accessible by any piece of software capable of resolving URLs, using the HTTP protocol and of interpreting HTML documents.

We can visualize the Web as a graph (Chap. 3). Any HTML document is a node. Links are arcs going from the node/page containing them to any other node/page. Figure 4.3 shows the Web as a graph in the middle. The various pages are stored on one of the many computers forming the Web, which means having a database or file system storing the pages, a Web browser that understands HTTP, and a URL to address the server and all the pages that it can provide. The Web browser is then a lens that gives a view of a page and its links. Following the links, the lens moves across/surfs the Web. The user perceives the system as one integrated hypertextual repository, but actually the browser is interacting with many independent machines to obtain the information.

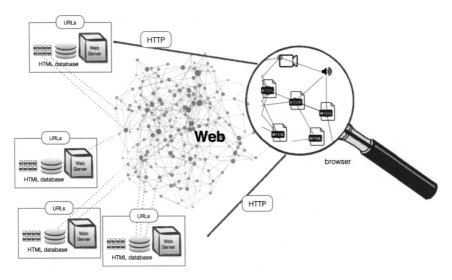

Fig. 4.3 The browser in the Web pattern

4.1   Uniform Resource Locator

The Uniform Resource Locator (URL) is a system for identifying resources on a network. It follows the general format of a Uniform Resource Identifier (URI):

$$\texttt{scheme: [//[user[:password]@]host[:port]] [/]}$$
$$\texttt{path[?query] [\#fragment]}$$

The `scheme` identifies the protocol to be used for accessing the resource; in the Web's case that is `http`, though it can also be `ftp`, `mailto`, `file`, `ssh`, and one of many others. The `user` part is usually not employed for basic Web interactions, but typically used for accessing resources requiring a login, such as a secure file transfer (sftp). The `host` is the name or IP address of the machine hosting the resource. A `port` is a unique identifier of a receiving process at the host end. For the Web, the default value is 80 and is typically omitted in the URLs. For secure connections, the protocol is `https` and the port 443. A `path` provides the relative location of the resource on the host; it usually looks like a hierarchical directory and file descriptor. It is possible to add parameters to the resource request. This is done via the `?query` part of the URL.

URLs were built on top of domain names, the subject of a set of RFCs in the early 1980s. As such, they inherit the advantages and disadvantages of the *Domain Name System (DNS)*. DNS is a distributed database for resolving names into IP addresses. Names are hierarchically organized, starting with a high level indicator of the country or organization (e.g., .com, .org, .gov, .edu, .mx, .it, .nl) and further specializations. The databases offer no consistency guarantees, and updates are propagated in a lazy fashion. However, given that changes to names are not frequent, this is not a major problem. Names can be resolved recursively or iteratively. One resolution instance can lead to a set of queries to DNS servers. The default transport protocol of DNS is UDP. Changing the name structure is difficult. Imagine that Mexico conquers the United States. Merging each government's .gov and .mx addresses so that existing URLs keep working would be anything but straightforward to implement.

Uniform Resource Locators were part of the initial Web prototype and have been standardized in RFC 1738, authored by Tim Berners-Lee in 1994. He later regretted the inclusion of the // in the URL, as he considered it redundant.

As an example, consider a locator for a page about Moby Dick and whales. The following could be the URL used, http://www.mobydickwhales.net:80/ swhale.html. The URL states that there is a file called "swhale.html" available on the machine, "www.mobydickwhales.net" is accessible via the http protocol, and the machine accepts "http" connections for this resource on port 80.

4.2   HyperText Transfer Protocol

The HyperText Transfer Protocol (HTTP) is a stateless request-reply protocol. For every resource that the client requests, the server will reply with information about the answer and, possibly, the resource. It is an application-level protocol that requires transportation on a lower-level protocol, which typically is the connection-oriented TCP.

A request consists of a header and the main payload of the message. The header is organized in the following way:

```
method URI [request_header] HTTP_version
```

The HTTP method specifies the nature of the request. GET and POST are the most commonly used methods. Their function is to receive a resource, or provide parameters for a request, such as using a Web form, respectively. Other methods are part of the protocol, such as PUT, DELETE, and OPTIONS. These methods are seldom implemented, as one does not want a random user to start deleting resources from a Web server. However, they show the original intention of the Web: a trustworthy, autonomous community with a simple interaction protocol. The URI is defined as described in the URL section above. The `request_header` is an optional field to provide additional information such as the accepted character encodings, the user-agent identifying the type of browsers used, and so on. The last field specifies the version of HTTP used.

The syntax of the response is similarly divided into two sections.

```
HTTP_version status reason [response_header] body
```

The reply announces the version of the protocol used; then it provides a `status` code. The status code is a three-digit number where 200 indicates a successful request, 404 is the famous (file) not found, while codes in the 500s indicate a server error. The `reason` is a textual explanation of the reason for returning the given code. `response_header` is an optional field to provide additional information such as age, location, time after which to retry, etc. The `body` section is what contains the actual data related to the request.

Going back to the whale example, the URL at which the page is available could be http://www.mobydickwhales.net/swhale.html. Passing it to the browser will generate a HTTP GET request to www.mobydickwhales.net and request the resource swhale.html. The server will reply with code 200 and transfer the html file with text, links, and a link to an image to embed into the page. To get the image, another HTTP request will be sent to the server. If there were 100 images, there would have to be 100 requests. These are independent requests and can travel on separate TCP sockets. If one decides to follow a link that goes to another page on the same website, a new request has to be sent.

The example gives an impression of the simplicity of the protocol. This allows it to be easy to implement, fast, portable, and scalable. However, there is very little semantics to an interaction, and no way to relate multiple interactions via the HTTP protocol. HTTP is the subject of multiple RFCs, namely, RFC 2068, RFC 2616, and RFC 7230 to 7237.

4.3   HyperText Markup Language

The HyperText Markup Language (HTML) is a textual format for annotating plain text with information relative to the formatting of the text and links to other files, including other HTML documents. It is openly based on the *Standard Generalized Markup Language (SGML)*, which was widely in use at CERN in the 1980s. SGML is a language that became an ISO standard in 1986 and whose origin can be traced to IBM's *Generalized Markup Language (GML)* developed in the 1960s. The original idea of HTML is to have two parts of a document: a header section with metadata and the actual hypertextual part. The distinction between text and markup is given by using angular brackets to surround markups: ⟨markup_statement⟩.

```
doctype head body
```

To show the basic structure of an HTML document, consider again the whale page. We located it with the URL http://www.mobydickwhales.net/swhale.html, and the browser retrieved it via a HTTP GET request. The content of the swhale.html file is:

```
<!DOCTYPE html>
<html>
  <head>
    <title>Sperm Whales</title>
  </head>
  <body>
    <p>The sperm whale, the biggest toothed whale.</p>
    <p>Moby Dick is a sperm whale.</p>
    <p><img src="spermWhale.jpg"></p>
    <p><a href="http://www.mobydickwhales.net">Home</a></p>
  </body>
</html>
```

The heading contains a title. This could be displayed in the browser head-bar or tab. The body starts with a textual paragraph marked by opening and closing tags <p> </p>, respectively. The third paragraph contains an image. The image is located on the same host and subdirectory; it requires a new HTTP connection to be downloaded. The source address spermWhale.jpg is equivalent to http://www.mobydickwhales.net/spermWhale.jpg. The last paragraph contains a link connected to the word Home. Most browsers will display such text differently from ordinary text or have the cursor change shape when it goes over it. If acted upon, the browser will perform a new HTTP connection to the URL in the href field and possibly display a new page.

HTML was part of the original Web proposal of Tim Berners-Lee, who built the first editor and browser for it. The first proposal for its precise definition is dated 1993, while a standard appeared in 1995 as HTML 2.0 in RFCs 1866 and 1867. The latest standardized version is HTML 5, standardized in 2014. HTML 5 offers the direct embedding of audio, video, and other graphical forms. It also has provisions for geo-localization and local data storage. In doing so, unlike its preceding versions, it deviates from the SGML standard, not being fully compatible with its mandates.

HTML is thus a language for the formatting of documents which provides information on the role of textual components in the document by declaring their function (e.g., a title, a header, running text) or directly stating how to display them (e.g., bold, italic, text color). The browser has some freedom in deciding how to display the text, given the markups. Such a way of defining documents is antithetic to the popular tools we are used to, such as Microsoft's Word. Word is part of the family of *What You See Is What You Get (WYSIWYG)* systems, where the editor's view and the final document look coincide. While WYSIWYG helps the user to have an immediate idea of the aspect of a document, and allows for direct manipulation of the graphics, it does give problems of portability and of abstractions. It is sometimes also referred to as *What You See Is All You Get.*

The present book has been typeset using LATEX, a text processing system based on compiling an instruction language.[1] LATEX is often referred to as a markup language and therefore compared to HTML. This is a bit of a stretch. HTML is an interpreted language: one of its documents can be displayed in a multitude of ways, but it is not possible to specify macros or arithmetic expressions in it. On the contrary, LATEX is a compiled language, and its goal is that, independently of where it is compiled, the output will always look the same. Furthermore, one can write arithmetic expressions to control the layout and contents of the document. The expressions, together with all macros, are evaluated at compile time.

HTML's success as the document format of the Web also brought popularity to SGML and has often been referred to the prototypical example of SGML. In fact, the growing use of the Web had made developers, but also generic Web users, familiar with the bracket-based markups <>. Tim Berners-Lee was a strong advocate of the idea that browsers should also be HTML editors, though the feature was most often not implemented and writing HTML documents manually without a specific tool was not too

---

[1] LATEX is Leslie Lamport's extension to Donald Knuth's TEX, which was released in 1978.

uncommon in the early days of the Web. As users were getting accustomed to the markup style, it felt natural to use the SGML-like descriptors beyond Web pages and for marking up data more generally. The tags are human-readable and, if validated for consistency against an abstract data specification, can be useful for the interoperation of computers. The trend became concrete with the definition of a generic markup language based on the principles of SGML and derived from HTML's popularity, the *eXtensible Markup Language (XML)*. Soon after its introduction, this language became rapidly accepted and used. "The XML revolution that followed has been greeted with great enthusiasm, even by the SGML community, since it keeps the principles of SGML in place. When Tim Bray, editor of the XML specification, waved it at the attendees at the WWW6 conference in April 1997, he was greeted with applause—because the spec was thin enough to wave" [19]. Having a platform-independent data format, equipped with a data validation mechanism, promised to solve the interoperation problems of a connected world—Something that a decade earlier was addressed by middleware layers, possibly object-oriented, such as CORBA. We will look into CORBA in Sect. 7.2.

XML is indeed a flexible and portable solution to data representation. It has features of human readability and ease of transportation over a network. To be fair, it also has some drawbacks, most notably its verbosity. Replying to a request with a yes or no can take tens of tags and several bytes of a message, where literally one bit of information could have been enough.

5

The Browser Lament
And the Browser Wars

Gentlemen, you can't fight in here; this is the war room!
Dr. Strangelove, S. Kubrick

"If you reinvented the wheel, you would get your wrist slapped for not reading. But nowadays people are reinventing the flat tire. I'd personally be happy if they reinvented the wheel, because at least we'd be moving forward." In the 2012 interview, Alan Kay provides some arguments about what he finds flawed about the Web. The main problem, according to him, is its exclusive focus on hypertextuality and distribution, while ignoring entirely the computational ability of the components involved. He mentions Engelbart's pioneering work and HyperCard as examples of what the original Web design entirely overlooked (see Chap. 3). Kay says, "If they reinvented what Engelbart did, we'd be way ahead of where we are now. [...] HyperCard was 1989. Find me Web pages that are even as good as HyperCard."[1]

---

[1]HyperCard was actually released in 1987.

© Springer International Publishing AG, part of Springer Nature 2018
M. Aiello, *The Web Was Done by Amateurs*,
https://doi.org/10.1007/978-3-319-90008-7_5

5.1   The Browser Is an Application

The original Web pattern is just about the exchange of static documents and making sure that these can be interpreted at any end. The core technologies proposed by Tim Berners-Lee are simply about the formatting of multimedia documents, and their localization and transfer. If this is the setting, it is only natural that the browser, as depicted in Fig. 4.3, is an application running on top of the operating system of the computer. The browser takes advantage of the networking system calls available in the operating system, of the computational power of the host to interpret HTML documents, and of the operating system graphic packages to render Web pages interactively. The problem lies in the possibility of making computations part of the Web navigation. What if one wants to learn about the Logo programming language and run an example? In the Web pattern there are no provisions for embedding instructions and execution specifications into an HTML page and letting them execute in remote machines based on the user context. It is like having a microscope to observe the microscopic world versus having a full-fledged chemical lab. One can look around the Web like in a Petri dish with a microscope, but one cannot influence what one sees by adding chemical reactants to the dish.

The browser's lack of computational ability is at the core of Kay's criticism. He states, "You want it to be a mini-operating system, and the people who did the browser mistook it as an application." In other terms, the Web seems to exist outside of the computers connecting to it, as a multi-media database. The application-browser allows users to jump from link to link, but not to execute locally. The browser application relies on the operating system for all its basic functionality, and its computational needs are met by local system calls. The browser can merely ask for help in interpreting HTML tags and using a graphical user interface.

On the other hand, if the browser was an operating system, it would have full access to all the resources of a computer. When accessing a page on Logo, it could simply interpret Logo statements and provide, as part of that navigation, the output of the program. The page could then be a mixture of textual information, links to other resources, and code. All of these would have uniquely specified semantics, meaning that they would execute in the same way, modulo context specific personalizations, on all machines.

In the next chapter, we will see patches to the original design of the Web that move it towards the operating system, but these are indeed patches. One of them is the introduction of Java applets to Web pages. This basically requires the inclusion of a small operating system (the virtual machine) in the bowser to provide semantically standard execution across browsers. But before we look into these aspects, consider the history of Web browsers, as they had a central role in bringing innovation to the Web with novel ideas and necessary extensions.

5.2   Early Browsers

HTML is a language that "declares" properties and layout information of hypertextual documents. It is up to the browser to interpret these and make decisions on how to let the user enjoy the information. The browser is not a fixed piece of software, but something open that anybody can develop for their uses. The first browser was realized by Tim Berners-Lee himself in 1989. Many more soon followed.

WorldWideWeb Browser

Tim Berners-Lee developed the first browser prototype in 1989, which he also called `WorldWideWeb`. He built it on a NeXT machine that was acquired by CERN that year. The NeXT machine ran a version of the UNIX operating system and had powerful graphics. Beyond being the first browser, it also was the first HTML editor, providing a WYSIWYG approach to creating Web pages.

Lynx

The 1980s saw the passage from the large, shared machines to the personal computer and the wide availability of graphical user interfaces. Users were still accustomed to line-based shells and terminals to control their machines. In fact, most often these were the only interfaces available, as not everybody had access to a window-based operating system. Therefore, having a line-based browser was a good solution for most new entrants to the Web. Lynx was one of the first and best-known.

In Lynx, one would visualize the text of the HTML document in a shell, and underlined text or different colors would indicate that some terms were links that could be followed. The first Web page that ever went live at CERN is shown through the lens of Lynx in Fig. 5.1.

Fig. 5.1   The Lynx browser on the first CERN Web page

The Lynx browser on the swhale.html page is shown in Fig. 5.2. In Lynx there are no figures rendered inline, just text and links. The image of the whale is offered as a link for its download.

Mosaic

Tim Berners-Lee wanted the Web to succeed and understood the importance of the platform being embraced by as many developers and users as possible.

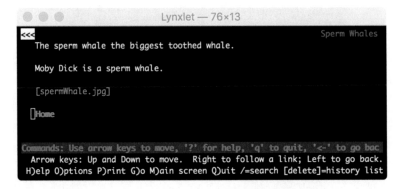

Fig. 5.2   The Lynx browser on the `swhale.html` page

To achieve this, he encouraged other people to build browsers and lobbied with CERN to share the platform copyright free. He was successful in both initiatives. In April 1992, the first web browser with embedded images and tables was released, `Viola`. It was the effort of a UC Berkeley student, Pei-Yuan Wei. In the same year, a group of Finnish master's students released a graphical browser called `OTHErwise`. One year later, CERN, referring to Lynx, the Web server, and relative code, announced that it would relinquish "all intellectual property rights to this code, both source and binary and permission is given to anyone to use, duplicate, modify and distribute it." All was released under the GNU General Public Licence (GPL).

Most browsers' efforts saw the personal involvement and encouragement of Berners-Lee. One of the most promising ones was that taking place at the *National Center for Supercomputing Applications (NCSA)* of the University of Illinois Urbana-Champaign. Tim Berners-Lee was involved and provided the initial help and support, though he felt the collaboration was going in the wrong direction. He noted, "The people at NCSA were attempting to portray themselves as the center of Web development, and to basically rename the Web as Mosaic. At NCSA, something wasn't 'on the Web,' it was 'on Mosaic.' Marc seemed to sense my discomfort at this." Marc Andreessen and Eric Bina had seen an early version of Viola and went on to develop the NCSA Web browser; this was called `Mosaic` and rapidly became the most popular browser, the first one ever to dominate an emerging market. A screenshot of Mosaic is shown in Fig. 5.3.

The commercial potential of Mosaic was clear to Andreessen who in fact left NCSA together with Bina to found a new company to commercialize the browser. Mosaic's last release dates January 1997.

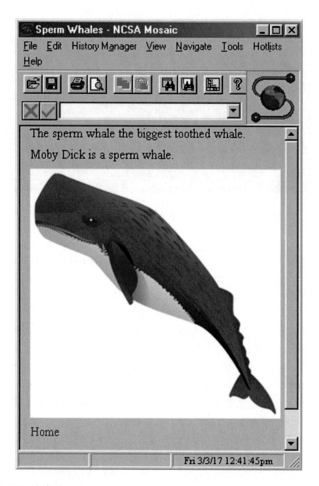

Fig. 5.3 The Mosaic browser

5.3   Netscape

Andreessen and Bina moved to the Silicon Valley to create Netscape, bringing with them a considerable amount of people from the NCSA Mosaic team. Even though they had no concrete earning model for their product when they started, the development of the browser went at full speed. The use of the Web as an eCommerce platform brought a number of important innovations. Netscape introduced the idea of saving data on the browser, called cookies (see Chap. 6), and of having a secure layer to protect the privacy and integrity of business transactions, the *Secure Socket Layer (SSL)*.

The first release of Netscape's browser, named Mozilla, dates October 1994. It became very popular and in a few years became the most used browser. Netscape marks the end of the research-project Web and the beginning of the commercial interest and exploitation period. Netscape struggled to find an appropriate business model. Nevertheless, the founders and investors cashed out in a big way. On August 9, 1995, the initial public offering (IPO) took place. The stock price doubled the expected one and went for $28 a share, touching as high as $75 a piece in the first day of trading. What was extraordinary back then was that Netscape had never made any profit. Still, investors were willing to take the risk. The IPO is considered the beginning of the financial frenzy around tech companies that fueled innovation and high gains in the 1990s. It is also seen as the beginning of the inflation of the dot-com bubble that burst in 2000. Netscape was acquired by American OnLine (AOL) in 1998. A screenshot from one of the last versions of Netscape is shown in Fig. 5.4.

5.4   Microsoft's Internet Explorer

Important economic interests often bring in aggressive players. The play can be so acrimoniously run that it leads to a war. And indeed this is what happened in the browser arena. It was clear that the Web was an emerging technology that had fantastic commercial potential. In the beginning, retail and online shopping were the most beaten routes for revenues. It didn't take long for the tech giant Microsoft to get interested in being part of the players, and with an exceptional capital, it was a player that could soon dominate. Microsoft's engagement in the competition with its Internet Explorer browser marked the beginning of the *First Browser War*.

Thomas Reardon, a project leader in the Windows 95 team, started working on a Web browser at Microsoft in 1994. He began alone and slowly attracted more staff to help him. They developed what was to become the first version of their browser on time to bundle it in the 1995 release of Windows; it was called `Internet Explorer`. Being a first basic release, it lacked most of the features of the market leader, Netscape. It was actually based on a third party browser created by a small company called Spyglass. In his blog, the head of the Spyglass browser project, Erik Sink, provides a nice historic reconstruction [105].

When Sink joined Spyglass, the company was focusing on scientific data analysis tools. In 1994, they started pursuing the Web as a potential new market. He lead the browser team. They licensed the Mosaic browser and

Fig. 5.4 The Netscape browser's latest version

trademarks, though soon developed their own engine for several platforms: Windows, MacOS, and Unix. Their competition and perhaps the first "mini-war" was with Netscape. Spyglass had a strong product and managed to license it to 120 customers, though Netscape was getting larger and larger portions of the user basis. Soon the development team at Netscape was ten times the size of Spyglass', thus developing a feature-rich product faster than any competitor.

By the end of 1994, Microsoft licensed Spyglass Mosaic for a quarterly fee plus a percentage of revenues for the software on third party products. This was a great success for Spyglass, though it also entailed the loss of all their other clients. Sink reports that "Internet Explorer 2.0 was basically Spyglass Mosaic with not too many changes. IE 3.0 was a major upgrade, but still largely based on our code. IE 4.0 was closer to a rewrite, but our code was still lingering around—we could tell by the presence of certain esoteric bugs that were specific to our layout engine." Microsoft had thus entered the browser competition fully and, as typical for Microsoft, as a late-comer. It was ready to battle Netscape. By the end of 1995, Microsoft was totally engaged as evidenced by Bill Gates announcing that Microsoft "was going to 'embrace and extend' the Internet." The announcement was a clear sign for Tim Berners-Lee, who noted, "To certain people in the computer industry, 'embrace' meant that Microsoft's products would start off being compatible with the rest of Web software, and 'extend' meant that sooner or later, once they had market share, Microsoft's products would add features to make other people's systems seem incompatible. Gates was turning the company around very rapidly and forcefully, to fully exploit the Web" [19].

Taking advantage of the market dominance of its operating system, Microsoft started bundling the Explorer browser into all releases of Windows. This had three effects: (1) instantly having a huge user base, (2) not having to pay fees to Spyglass for the browser since it was provided for free, (3) being able to push Microsoft's own standards or proprietary solutions. All three operations were possible because of the size and budget of Microsoft, though all three were controversial. On May 18, 1998, the United States Department of Justice and 20 states opened an investigation on abuse of monopoly on Microsoft's operating system and Web browser business. Further, Spyglass sued Microsoft on its avoidance of license fees and settled for $8 million on January 22, 1997.

The antitrust investigation ended with a settlement agreement almost four years later, on November 2, 2001. Microsoft was to share its application programming interfaces and have a committee assessing its procedures. Many have criticized the mild penalty and advantageous ruling in favor of Microsoft. This happened while Internet Explorer was raising in market share, almost reaching 100% of the user base by 2003–2004.

The war with Netscape was won. Netscape went out of business and was acquired by AOL, though before disappearing, it open sourced its product and launched a new player: `Mozilla FireFox`.

5.5   Google's Chrome

Despite being a late entrant, Google's Chrome browser is currently the "winner" of the browser war. First released in 2008, the browser is an open source project which runs on multiple operating systems, including several mobile ones, such as Android and iOS.

The browser has, and has had since its first release, very good performance in displaying pages, high compliance to Web standards, and reasonably strong security. Browsers do share navigation information with the Google company, unless set not to do so.

Rather than a new epic war, like the First Browser War, the Web has since seen many battles and the appearance of various new contenders. According to Marketshare.com, Internet Explorer has a very small share of the market today, about 5%, while Google's Chrome has over 50%, Apple's Safari about 15%, and Firefox 7%, and many others in the market split the rest. From the point of view of non-compliance with standards, Explorer is still the less compatible one, having only about half of the HTML 5 features implemented, while Chrome is at about 90% [113].

$$\sim$$

The browser provides an interpretation of the HTML pages that is not uniquely determined. To get an impression, compare the very same HTML page about whales rendered by three very different browsers: Figs. 5.2, 5.3, and 5.4. The browser can do so because the design of the Web intentionally wants to leave freedom to the end-point of the connection, that is, the browser, to guarantee fault-tolerance, among other things. The driving principle is that it is better to render something slightly differently than intended by the author of the document, rather than frustrating the user by showing nothing and returning an interpretation error. A very loose enforcement of document interpretation rules, and document semantics, is what may very well have helped the success of the Web by truly making it an open platform for all. At the same time, and here comes the critique of Kay, the platform is static in its moving computations and services around the Internet. The lack of an object-oriented definition—for instance, of the Web exchange units—makes uniformity, clear semantics, mobility of objects, and computations hard to achieve, if achievable at all.

The freedom in building the browser has enabled companies and non-profit communities to compete for the best product, to try to push for their own technology, and in the end to innovate the Web at a fast pace. It has also sparked several browser wars for market dominance (see Fig. 5.5). Netscape

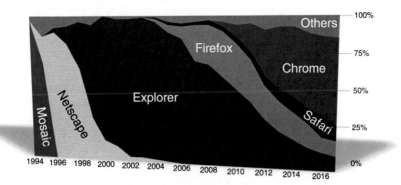

Fig. 5.5 Market share of browsers from 1994 to 2017 (multiple sources)

won over Mosaic, then lost to Explorer, who dominated for a decade. The most recent dominator is Chrome, who currently claims slightly more than half of the market.

Over time, the browser has come closer to the operating system. The functionality of browsing the Web has been similar to that of browsing file systems. Permanent storage has become more easily accessible from the browser, but these are just patches to the original Web design. The browser still is, today, an application-level software.

Part III

The Patches

6

Patching the Web
States and Objects

It's not a bug! It's a feature.
Anonymous

The Web is an evolving system. Its popularity and its openness have allowed and attracted a plethora of individuals, organizations, and companies to contribute to it—starting with Netscape introducing cookies and SSL, and moving on to the browser wars, the standardization panels, and the open source projects. This means that the Web of today is very different from that of 30 years ago, and its future will certainly bring many more innovations.[1] I focus here on the evolution of the Web, going from its origins as a document exchange system towards its gradual shift into a computational infrastructure. The claim of Kay is that even in 2012 the process was far from even reaching the quality of 1987's HyperCard, but at least it was going in that direction. Since the comment is centered on the computational aspects, I will consider the major changes to the Web that took it on the computational infrastructure journey.

I call such changes *patches*, as they are attempts to fix the original design of the Web. These patches have to do with the necessity of having stateful client-server interactions, the balancing of the computational load between the client and the server, and the need for the clients to perform computations that go

---

[1]The website http://www.evolutionoftheweb.com displays a magnificent visualization of the evolution of the Web from its origin until 2012, highlighting the browsers' lifespan, and the introduction of new standards and technologies.

© Springer International Publishing AG, part of Springer Nature 2018
M. Aiello, *The Web Was Done by Amateurs*,
https://doi.org/10.1007/978-3-319-90008-7_6

beyond the simple rendering of text and user input acquisition. The focus is thus on what I call "computational patches," which are distinct from the visual interactions and the security ones. Most notably, in the coming pages I do not discuss the introduction of *Cascading Style Sheets (CSS)* or *Scalable Vector Graphics (SVG)*. Similarly, I do not consider security patches: not SSL nor any of its following developments. For important as they may be, they do not add much to the computational nature of the Web. In addition, there are plenty of excellent textbooks on how to make Web interactions secure [12], and a similar amount on how to hack them [107].

Patch I. Cookies

Introduction Year	1994
Principle	Store bits of information on the browser.
Patch to	The session-less nature of HTTP.
Standardization	RFC 2109, RFC 2965, RFC 6265.
Status	Cookies are still widely used and have been the precursors of a family of techniques to store information across HTTP interactions on the client side [31]. By their very nature, they bring a number of security vulnerabilities and raise privacy concerns [107].
Related Techniques	URL parameters, JSON Web tokens, hidden form fields, Web storage, browser cache.

6.1   Patch I: Cookies

If the Web is a set of static pages interlinked with each other, any page access is a self-contained operation. One moves from page to page in a Markovian fashion, meaning that the rendering of any one document is not dependent on the previously visited one. This is why the underlying HTTP exchange protocol is stateless. There is no need to remember what page was just loaded to decide on how to render the next one. Or is there?

Consider two very different Web interactions. In one, the user is interested in learning more about sperm whales. After reading a page describing their biology, the user follows a link to Herman Melville's novel, in which they learn that Moby Dick is a whale of the sperm species. One could also go the other way around: first read about the novel and then go to the page on the biology of the mammal. These interactions do not require the remembering of any information regarding the sequence of pages visited, as shown in Fig. 6.1.

Now consider a case in which the user wants to buy Melville's book. First, they go to a page of an on-line bookstore. Then they search for the book, put it in the virtual cart, and press a button to perform the purchase. The next page that the user expects is the one to provide payment and shipment information. One expects that page to be about Melville's book, but wait, the book information was part of the previous Web page! Now we have a clear state dependency between the current page and the previous one: we are inside a transaction, or a session that spans over several Web pages (Fig. 6.2). For instance, one cannot jump from the second page to the last sent page, skipping the payment one, because it would bring the interaction into an inconsistent state with respect to the business logic of the application—that is, the shipping of a book for which no payment was received.

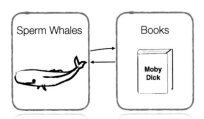

Fig. 6.1   Static Web pages about whales and books

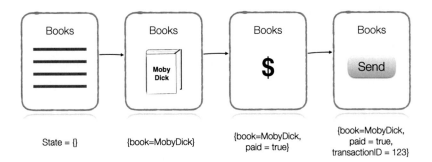

Fig. 6.2   A sequence of pages with an associated state

HTTP has no provisions for supporting sessions across pages. The session needs to be managed somehow outside the Web pattern (Chap. 5), or in other terms, one needs to store somewhere a state of the interaction between the client and the server, and keep updating that status as the interaction proceeds. One can design such a session management in a number of ways. One can keep status information on the server, though how can one make sure that the browser behaves consistently and does not reload the same page or jump to a random new one? Or what if the back button is pressed during a session and the user goes to another book; what is the user really buying? Another possibility is to embed status information into the URL. In the first page, one could add parameters to links that embed the status, something like http://bookshop.com/buy?book=MelvilleMD&copies=1. But again, having no control on the browser, the same incoherent behaviors such as hitting the back button can compromise the session.

The vision of an object "book" having the defined behavior of being bought and composing it with a payment object is not achievable, but one could at least try to create a notion of a session by storing the state of the interaction on both the server and the client ends. The server is in control of the HTML pages it provides, which in turn represent its state. On the client side, one needs the ability to store some information regarding the state of the session and possibly confirming it back to the server in the request for the next page. This leads to the first important computational patch: storing variable values on the client side, better known as *cookies*.

The term cookie has been used in the context of exchanging a token of information among networked Unix programs. The token helps identification of the interaction and is typically not directly used by the client. In this context, one talks of a "magic cookie" mimicking the Chinese fortune cookies that contain a message that is visible only after opening it [100]. In the Web's case, the cookie is used as a binding contract between client and server, where the client "remembers" information pertaining to the state of the transaction.

Cookies were introduced early on the Web, as it became evident that a mechanism for managing long-running sessions and transactions was necessary to enable on-line purchases. Louis Montulli, who built the Lynx browser and who was one of the first engineers hired by Netscape, devised the stateful mechanism for the browser. The request came from a client of Netscape who wanted to store on-line transaction information outside of their servers. The feature was added to the September 1994 browser release, and discussions on the specification of the cookies from Montulli started soon after, reaching the status of an agreed RFC, called HTTP State Management Mechanism, in 1997 [71]. As of today, all major browsers support cookies.

Patch II. Java

Introduction Year	1995
Principle	Fully object-oriented language, having a virtual machine running on the client and acting inside the browser.
Patch to	The inability of HTML to have executable instructions.
Standardization	None. Originally property of Sun Microsystems, and an open source since 2007.
Status	Java is a fully object-oriented, concurrent, and platform-independent programming language. It is widely used, especially for Web programming.
Related Techniques	ActiveX controls, Flash objects, Silverlight objects.

6.2   Patch II: Run Anywhere

Suppose that there is a high demand for a service counting how many instances of any word are in Melville's novel *Moby Dick*—a system that can say that the word "whale" is present 1.585 times in the 206.052-words novel. What makes the service interesting is that it can provide such a number for any word present in the book: "the" 19.408 times, "Ishmael" 20 times, and so on. How can we deliver such a service on the Web?

If we stick to the original Web pattern, we would have to store a page for every word appearing in the book and its respective word count (Fig. 6.3). This sounds like an unreasonable amount of pages. More effectively, we could write a program on the server that searches the book and counts the number of pages dynamically, generating an HTML page on demand for the request of any word. The program can be made more efficient by processing the book's text off-line and storing information about word occurrence in a reverse index file. One needs to store only the book on the server and execute some search code for any client request. Building a client-server interaction that entails the execution of a program for every client request became one of the first ways to bring dynamic content to Web pages. Not static stored HTML pages, but rather pages generated on demand. *Common Gateway Interfaces (CGI)* were first used by NCSA in 1993 and have since been a viable solution for dynamic content generation (Fig. 6.4). The main problem, though, is scalability. If a

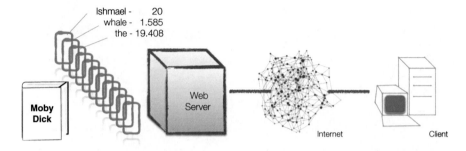

Fig. 6.3 A page per request approach

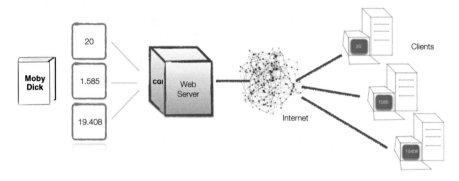

Fig. 6.4 Common gateway interface approach

server receives many requests concurrently, it has to start many processes at the same time, one per request, and its resources will not be able to cope with a growth in demand.

Scalability is achievable by better balancing the load of the computation between the client and the server. The server could provide, rather than a dynamically generated Web page, instructions on how to generate the page, as in Fig. 6.5. This is especially useful if the client is going to execute a number of requests of the same nature but with different parameters, e.g., how many occurrences of "whale"? how many of "black" and "ship" together? The original idea of a Web browser is that of simply interpreting HTML tags, not understanding instructions such as those of a programming language.

Java was launched in 1995 by Sun Microsystems. It is an object-oriented programming language that comes with a full specification of the machine it will run on. In other terms, its programs are not compiled for specific computers, but for an abstract machine that is independent of the platform.

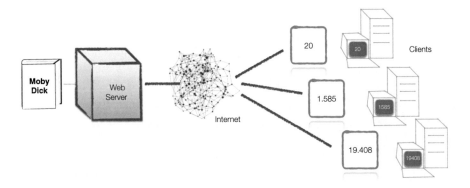

Fig. 6.5　Offloading the computation to the clients

This is called the *Java Virtual Machine (JVM)*. The JVM is fully specified and can be installed on any computer. The idea is to make the programs machine-independent and let the peculiarities of every hardware be handled at the level of the JVM.

Java programs are compiled into standard bytecode instructions that are then interpreted by the Java Virtual Machine. The approach has been marketed from its beginning as "Write Once, Run Anywhere," giving the hope of a headache-less deployment of applications across platforms. Unfortunately, the JVM has not been uniformly implemented by all hardware vendors, and the motto has been sometimes mockingly rephrased into "Write Once, Debug Everywhere."

Java comes from the inventive mind of James Gosling from Sun. He worked on the Java programming language, originally called Oak, for four years before its launch. The original target was that of digital television and home appliances. That is, Java was intended as a platform for portable and platform-independent applications. In 1995, with the emergence of the Web, Sun decided to retarget the product and use Java to bring computation to the Web's clients. The name Java comes from the preferred coffee beans of the development team at Printers Inc. coffee shop in downtown Palo Alto, a regular hangout for the team and many other techies of the area till its closing in 2001.

The combination of Java with the Web relies on making the JVM available to the browser on the client side. Together with a Web page, the server sends compiled Java code, the bytecodes, and links them with a newly defined HTML tag. Such a code is known as an *Applet*. When the browser hits that tag, it invokes an instance of the JVM and gives it the bytecodes for execution. The JVM used on the Web page has some limitations, though. It has a specific area of the Web page assigned to it for its graphical output and can perform a limited number of operations, e.g., it cannot freely access the file system of the host computer. The idea of limiting the execution of the JVM is known as *sandboxing*. Like a child in a sandbox who can play with the sand but not go outside the box, the JVM in a browser can compute and provide limited graphical interaction, but it cannot use the file system, access the network, or start new processes.

Going back to the word count example, the Web server sends a generic page together with a Java applet that has in its memory the word list of the book. Any request for a word count or combination of them results in a computation local to the client, and no use of the network or other server resources (Fig. 6.5).

In designing a Web application there is always tension on where to put the load of the computation and, to some extent, the data. The approach of doing as much as possible on the server goes under the name of having *thin clients*. In its extreme form, the client does just graphics rendering and accepts input from user interaction, while all the computation is done on the server. When hardware was more expensive than today, the vision of thin clients had more followers. In the mid-1990s, Sun's slogan was "The Network is the Computer," and they had a product line of thin clients. The slogan, originally proposed by employee number 21 of Sun, John Gage, is still popular today as we see the emergence of Edge Computing (Sect. 7.9) [51].

On the other end of the spectrum is the idea that the load of the interaction mostly relies on the client, the *fat client* approach. In this way, the server can scale and provide functionalities to more clients, while the clients can be more responsive to the user, avoiding delays that are due to network latencies. The trend of powerful hardware at reasonable costs on mobile and embedded devices makes the fat client approach workable and economically attractive.

When launched, Java was an instant success, and still is a very popular programming language with almost ten million active programmers today. It is also used as a language for teaching programming in many academic and professional institutions.

Patch III. JavaScript

Introduction Year	1995
Principle	Embed commands into HTML to be executed on the client.
Patch to	The lack of commands for governing the client side's behavior at page interpretation time.
Standardization	ECMA International: ECMAScript-262, ECMAScript version 2 through 5.1, ECMAScript 2016.
Status	JavaScript is widely used for Web pages, and also on the server side (e.g., Node.js). It is also used in PDF documents.
Related Techniques	PHP, Visual Basic Script, JScript, ActionScript.

6.3   Patch III: Scripting

While cookies bring state information to the client, and Java brings a container for the controlled execution of objects, developers soon felt the need for another computational patch. It was necessary to put instructions inside HTML files to be executed by the browser while interpreting and rendering the Web pages. This would bring HTML closer to LaTeX in its expressivity potential.

The need for such client side expressivity sprouted early at Netscape, more or less at the same time as cookies and Java were being integrated into the browser. Brendan Eich was recruited by Netscape with the goal of developing its first scripting language. LiveScript was released together with the September 1995 version of Netscape and three months later renamed JavaScript to align with the licensing of Java from Sun.

The JavaScript language was used as one of the weapons of the browser wars (Chap. 5), with the various contenders coming up with their own languages or dialects of JavaScript. Microsoft initially pushed for Visual Basic Scripting in 1996. Later it promoted its own JavaScript version as part of Dynamic HTML, and till the early 2000s it was implementing incompatible versions in its Internet Explorer browser. Netscape led an effort for standardization, putting its coordination in the hands of ECMA International, an evolution of the European Computer Manufacturers Association. This, though, was mostly ignored by the other players, Microsoft in particular.

The idea of JavaScript is that of embedding commands into HTML. Consider a dynamic version of our whale example listed on page 48, where some part of the text appears only after a button is clicked on the page itself.

```
<!DOCTYPE html>
<html>
  <head>
    <title>Sperm Whales</title>
  </head>
  <body>
    <p>The sperm whale, the biggest toothed whale.</p>
    <p>Moby Dick is a sperm whale.</p>

    <p id="image"><img src="spermWhale.jpg"></p>

    <button type="button"
     onclick='document.getElementById("image").innerHTML =
     "An image"'>Click here</button>
  </body>
</html>
```

The page displays the two paragraphs about sperm whales, the image of the whale, and a button at the end of the page. When the user presses the button, the image disappears and is substituted by the text "An image." Pressing the button does not trigger any interaction with the server; it is just a change in the presented page dictated by a local action.

JavaScript is a loosely typed, prototype-based, object-oriented programming language. It is embedded into HTML pages, and its commands are not displayed by the browser but rather interpreted. Object classes are not declared, but defined when the first prototype of an object is used. Prototypes can be changed at execution time by JavaScript instructions. Scoping of variables also has exceptions, called closures, that is, the transformation of a global variable into a local, private one. In less technical terms, JavaScript is a horrible example of an object-oriented language, full of exceptions that can help make a quick fix, but can render a program unreadable and unmaintainable.

Despite these design issues, JavaScript is very popular to date, and there are a number of good reasons for this. First of all, it does not require any extra plug-ins on the browsers. It is light to transport. It travels inside HTML in the same HTTP connection used to access the page. Being widely used for the client-side scripting, interpretation engines for it, supporting frameworks, and tools for developers have reached very good speeds and effectiveness, making it a good development choice. Furthermore, there are now server side tools also based on JavaScript, so it is possible to build a complete solution with a database (MongoDB), a server (Node.js), and a client (any major browser) using just JavaScript and one data format (JSON).

JavaScript was so much appreciated in the early days of the Web that it even drove the definition of a data formatting language. Founded in 2001, State Software had the goal to build a Web-based platform having an abstraction layer for Web development. This included a data exchange format. The idea was to use JavaScript object definitions to transport information between two collaborating hosts. The goal was also achieved by keeping two HTTP connections open between the two hosts, acting jointly as a kind of application level socket. The data format took the name of *JavaScript Object Notation (JSON)* and is to the credit of Douglas Crockford, one of the founders of State Software.

The paradigm of using JavaScript, JSON, and Node.js has reached such levels of popularity among developers in recent years that building Web applications that resemble self-contained applications is now done as a single Web page. That is, all the application logic is coded into one single HTML page. In this way, the response speed of the page is very high and all interactions are contained in one browser tab. The server then becomes only responsible for the permanent data storage, authentication, and validation. "When a user navigates through a traditional website, the server burns lots of processing power to generate and send page after page of content to the browser. The Single Page Application server is quite different. Most of the business logic— and all of the HTML rendering and presentation logic—is moved to the client. The server remains important, but it becomes leaner and more focused on services like persistent data storage, data validation, user authentication, and data synchronization" [90].

The popularity of JavaScript certainly had a boost in 2005, when Jesse James Garrett published a paper describing a set of JavaScript-based techniques for asynchronous content downloading in a Web page, abstracting from how Google Maps and Google Suggest had been designed [52]. *Asynchronous JavaScript+XML (AJAX)*, as the name suggests, uses a combination of JavaScript, XML data encoding, and HTTP asynchronous communication to provide Web pages that not only are dynamically generated, but whose content can be updated while on the user's browser. The HTTP variant used here is called *XMLHttpRequest*. It was originally introduced by Microsoft into Internet Explorer version 5.0 in 1999. It basically allows the browser to request XML documents and use the retrieved data in an already downloaded page. Slowly, all other browsers started implementing the library for supporting the protocol. As an example, the autocompletion feature of Web forms works thanks to this mechanism.

The power of having modular components that can be downloaded asynchronously and used in a Web page is so strong that AJAX can be considered a patch to the original Web design in itself. Since it is not a new technology, but rather a set of patterns and good practices, I decided to present it as part of the client side scripting patch.

What comes even closer to being a new patch is the proposal of *WebSockets*. Going beyond the possibility of making additional HTTP requests within a browser visualization, as in the case of XMLHttpRequest, with WebSockets the client and the server keep an open, bidirectional channel. The novelty lies in the fact that the communication is bidirectional, so the server can now push information towards the client, allowing for real-time content displaying. There is more: not having to perform an HTTP request-reply for every new resource means also saving bandwidth and reducing latency times. In fact, sending a boolean value may require just a few bytes rather than a full single HTTP connection worth several kilobytes, which reduces the latency by as much as three times [83].

The discussion about WebSockets occurred within the development of HTML 5 and was initially referred to as TCPConnection. The first version of the protocol appeared in 2008 and was supported by Google Chrome in late 2009. It finally made it as a stable IETF protocol as RFC 6455 in 2011.

The protocol is an important improvement over former techniques to provide bidirectional communication. These included polling and long-polling cycles where browsers kept requesting resources from the server, providing the possibility of continuous updates. However, each request requires a full HTTP request-reply, and it may deliver no data if no updates are necessary. Flash sockets have also been used, but again they require the Flash plug-in to be available and started on the browser.

The need for bidirectionality in the client-server interaction had actually emerged much earlier in the context of information syndication. For websites that have rapidly changing information, the user can be notified of changes, rather than having to poll on a regular basis. The *RSS feeds* (RDF Site Summary, also known as Really Simple Syndication) was created by Dan Libby and Ramanathan V. Guha at Netscape and released to the public in 1999. It included elements from Dave Winer's news syndication format. A mini-patch in itself, RSS was fixing the problem of dynamic and rapid change in Web pages' content, especially news Web pages and blogs. It has been largely superseded by the more powerful techniques mentioned above, though software supporting it still exists.

~

Cookies, Java, JavaScript, and, more generally, the three related patches do not satisfy Alan Kay's vision of a Web of well-defined traveling object instances. At most, these provide for some forms of mobility of computation on the existing Web infrastructure. His vision of a Web exclusively made of objects and composed at run-time, goes well-beyond such computational patches. He says, "What you really want is objects that are migrating around the net, and when you need a resource, it comes to you." What we've got on the Web, after the three major patches, is phantoms of objects that are either jailed inside a Java Virtual Machine or leave small traces of their passages as cookie crumbs here and there. Not the desired object exchanger. We still do not have the "browser" that Kay envisioned: a user interface that allows the interaction with object instances and the composition of objects in order to achieve interesting, complex, distributed behaviors.

7

Patch IV: Web Services
Web*

These days everything is Web-something.
Bill Gates

The fourth patch comes from the emerging need to use the Web differently—the need for not only a Web of information for humans, but a computational infrastructure for humans and other software systems. If one can access a page about stock quotes, why not let a computer program do the same and then perform some buys or sells on behalf of a user? This requires moving from a Web of human-readable pages to a Web of programmatically accessible nodes. This shift brought us the set of technologies known as Web Services. First, we consider the context in which these technologies sprouted and pre-Web ancestor CORBA. Then we look into the main pattern behind Web Services, the publish-find-bind pattern. And finally, I provide a personal tale regarding Web Service research.

7.1   Securing the Intranet

At the turn of the millenium, having a Web server as a front-end to the information system of a company or organization was becoming the common practice, almost independently of the company's size and ICT literacy level. This also meant that more and more nodes on the Internet could talk HTTP and have open connections on port 80, the standard access point for Web

© Springer International Publishing AG, part of Springer Nature 2018
M. Aiello, *The Web Was Done by Amateurs*,
https://doi.org/10.1007/978-3-319-90008-7_7

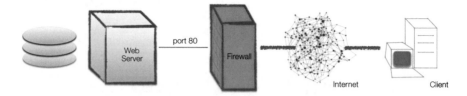

Fig. 7.1 Adding a firewall to allow only port 80 connections

page requests. In fact, the typical architecture in use at the end of the 1990s was a slightly more elaborate version of the three-tier architecture presented in Fig. 4.2 with a client, a server, and a database behind it. However, there was one additional component to this new version, designed to protect the internal ICT infrastructure: the *firewall*. The firewall filters out all undesired incoming requests, for instance, those coming to ports reserved only for internal invocations (Fig. 7.1). The main goal is to protect the internal ICT infrastructure of an organization, what is often referred to as the Intranet of a company. Most firewalls remain open only for Web requests that, in principle, can come from any node of the Internet. Businesses that needed to open frequent communication channels between their information systems could now use the standard HTTP Web connection as a channel, or better a tunnel, to allow messages to flow. An open opportunity for inter-organizational ventures was suddenly available, as information systems became more easily interoperable. In addition, new businesses could take advantage of existing services and compose them to provide an added value, complex service.

7.2   Corba and IDLs

Consider the integration of a book selling service with a payment service, or matching a real estate offering website with a map service and city council statistics. Or consider the integration of the information systems of two separate banks that decided to merge their operations. All these situations require specialized integration platforms and a great deal of expert work. In the mid-1990s, the *Common Object Request Broker Architecture (CORBA)* was considered the state-of-the-art solution. In 1998, the prominent *Communications of the ACM* journal had a special issue on CORBA presented as the middleware of the future [103]. The gist of the argument was as follows: the world is fully embracing object-oriented programming, just look at the recently introduced

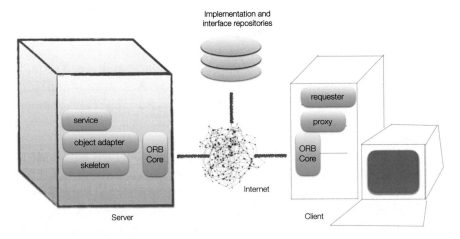

Fig. 7.2 The CORBA architecture

Java; we have the Internet as a communication medium; therefore, CORBA is the middleware for letting all information systems talk to each other. The editor of the special issue, Krishnan Seetharaman, concludes, "The furious pace at which the Internet and the World-Wide Web are growing requires a technological leap that can be provided by CORBA. [...] CORBA and Java complement each other and provide a powerful new paradigm for software development."

CORBA is a middleware for letting processes on separate machines interoperate independently of the programming language and basing the interaction on an object-oriented abstraction. Say that a program on a client wants to talk to a server. The CORBA middleware locally translates its request into a method invocation, sends it over, and the server translates the request from its object representation to the one used by its software and replies back (Fig. 7.2). The middleware provides a repository of available interfaces—that is, what can be invoked on available services—and a repository of available implementations, meaning where the interfaces are active and available for invocation, a kind of phone book for objects. The client must run the CORBA middleware and its ORB core, which provides access to the repositories, handles the request-reply protocol, and converts the local calls into global CORBA valid ones. A client program will make a local call to the CORBA middleware. This will create a proxy, and the proxy translates the call into a remote method invocation in the CORBA standard. The invocation can now go to the ORB core and be transmitted to the server. The server similarly implements the ORB core. When a request arrives, it goes to an object adapter that calls the servants. A skeleton local to the server makes the actual invocation. That is, it takes the remote method call and it translates it into a local server invocation [42].

What made CORBA promising was its language independence. The middleware would work for any object-oriented language. Actually, it would work for any language as long as the messages were abstracted as object invocations. To do so, the description of the objects has to follow a standard *Interface Definition Language (IDL)*.

Despite all its promises, CORBA never really conquered the sector. Michi Henning identifies a number of reasons for the failure of CORBA [60]. The lack of an accepted and implemented object model, the difficulties of writing CORBA code beyond simple examples, the inability to integrate with emerging Web technologies, and the lack of support for security and versioning, have all contributed to relegating CORBA to a niche tool. Henning also discusses the procedural and political backgrounds that have led to the technical difficulties hindering a widespread adoption. However, CORBA is emblematic of a technological need of the time, and its history is also a powerful premise for rethinking the Web. It serves as a cautionary tale, as Kay's idea of a Web of moving objects and distributed object loaders should hope not to fall into the same pitfalls CORBA did.

7.3   The Magic Triangle

CORBA failed to deliver the omnipresent solution for enterprise integration, but it nevertheless paved the way towards its achievement. The idea of decoupling clients of objects from their containers was there, as was the idea of using standardized languages, and the increasing availability of Internet connections was a given. What was missing was just a simple and portable solution. The success of the Web and the emergence of XML as the Lingua Franca for data representation provided the right platforms for a new solution to take off.

The first step in such a direction was the release of the *Simple-Object Access Protocol (SOAP)* in 1998. As the name suggests, the protocol is a simple XML schema that defines how to carry a message with a method request. Inside, one could route any type of object invocation, including a CORBA one. The success of the protocol is tied to its attempt to minimize, insofar as it is possible within the XML bounds, the amount of overheads for a request. SOAP is an application-level protocol that can travel on any other transfer mechanism. Typically, it is embedded in HTTP, but it can also be placed in an email and thus travel over an email protocol such as SNMP, making SOAP both firewall friendly and flexible to other specific needs, as in the case of email delivery.

SOAP rapidly received the attention of the community, and the following step was to fill the need of a specific interface definition language for Web interaction. This followed a couple of years later with the proposal of a dedicated Interface Definition Language, the *Web Service Description Language (WSDL)*. The protocol describes object operations and procedures to be invoked remotely and the way in which these can be assembled into messages for a server. The description is composed of an abstract part that can be implemented by any server and a concrete part with actual links to existing implementations, expressed in terms of URLs. Many XML protocol proposals followed, addressing various aspects of the client-server interaction, including workflows spanning over several operations with IBM's *Web Service Flow Language (WSFL)*, created by Frank Leymann in 2001, and security (*WS-Security*, 2002). A new set of protocols, technologies, and development patterns was rapidly emerging.

These efforts both came from and attracted an increasing number of corporate and small-time developers, and they deserved a collective name. Around the turn of the century, a number of senior engineers and top executives met to discuss technology, standardization, and cooperation. During that meeting there was wide consensus on the fact that distributed units were increasing in granularity and size and could be considered *services*. XML was the common language for the interactions and the Internet the medium for their exchange. Now the problem was to give a name to that family of protocols and technologies to make them recognizable and widely successful. During that meeting, Bill Gates said, "We should call them Web Services. These days everything is Web-something."[1]

One of the Web Service standards that showed much promise was the *Universal Description, Discovery, and Integration (UDDI)* originally launched in 2000. The idea of the UDDI is to have a federation of registries where Web Services can be found. The registry is organized in three sections: white pages with contact information of service providers, yellow pages relating the service offerings to taxonomy relevant for the federation, and green pages with technical information about the services exposed, expressed in terms of WSDL. UDDI can assist the decoupling of service requesters from service providers. When a program needs a functionality, it accesses a UDDI relevant to its federation, retrieves technical information about the service it needs, and

---

[1]This was relayed to me firsthand by someone present at the meeting, who prefers remaining anonymous.

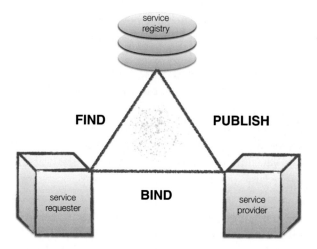

Fig. 7.3 The publish-find-bind pattern

obtains a list of suitable providers. It can then contact the provider, embedding a WSDL request into a SOAP envelope and letting it travel on HTTP over the Internet. The decision on which object to invoke can thus be deferred as late as execution time. One can decide which specific service to invoke just in time, when it is actually needed in the computation. Say that your program needs a function to compute square roots, and it does not have it on its local machine. One can write the program to access a specific library hosted on a known computer, or one can write a program that accesses a registry of available objects, passes on a description of the desired square root service, and retrieves back a list of available providers. Then it starts invoking them, either one by one or all at once, until it gets the computation it needed. This leads to a new way of developing systems and writing code, a way based on the *publish-find-bind* pattern. The pattern is best described as a triangle, as done in Fig. 7.3. Service providers *publish* their interfaces and availability in a registry. Service requesters search for these and possibly *find* them in that registry. The registry offers links to the service implementations made available by the providers so that the requester can then *bind* to the provider and execute the request.

The Web Service protocols just presented enable the pattern in the following way. UDDI acts as the registry for publishing and finding services. WSDL is the interface definition language to technically describe the services to be found, while SOAP acts as a wiring protocol to bind the client to the server [96]. Though Web Services are the prominent example of the

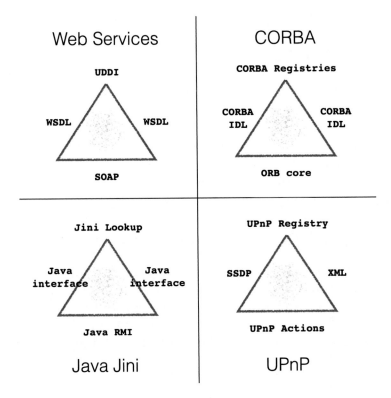

Fig. 7.4 Examples of technologies that enable the publish-find-bind pattern

publish-find-bind pattern, they are not the only and certainly not the first one. The idea of decoupling objects from their invokers and even finding them spontaneously at run-time has been the core of several technologies. Figure 7.4 shows four examples: Web Services, CORBA, Jini, and UPnP. Reconsidering Fig. 7.2, we notice the role of the CORBA registries in allowing late object binding, while the IDL and ORB cores of the specification provide means for object method description and binding, respectively.

Sun launched Jini in 1998 as part of Java. Jini enables Java Virtual Machines to act as registries, *lookups* in Jini terminology, for remote methods of objects contained in arbitrary Java Virtual Machines. The methods are described as Java interfaces. Lookup services are federated and distributed. A mechanism of leases allows lookup services to be up to date about available services, while broadcasting is used to find lookup services. Jini is thought of as a solution for pervasive computing, where a device joins a local network and can cooperate with other devices available. The typical example is someone entering a room with a camera which is Jini enabled. The camera discovers a screen service and a printing one, and seamlessly sends images to both for visualization and printing purposes.

Universal Plug and Play (UPnP) is a standard initially proposed by Microsoft in 1998 to allow the interconnection of devices and easy interoperation. Today it is governed by its own forum formed by several hundreds of vendors. UPnP is platform independent and makes heavy use of XML and message broadcasting. Devices offer and request sets of services that offer *actions*. UPnP uses an XML-based format to describe services and the relations among services, in a basic ontological form.

What's magic about the publish-find-bind triangle is that it allows a component to search for what it needs just-in-time, at the precise moment it needs it. The pattern goes as far as the possibility to design a component enabled to talk with other future components that do not even exist yet. Just think of designing a photo-camera that uses UPnP to print its images and then one day having it find, on an UPnP network, a sky-printing device that can render images in the sky for a square kilometer. As long as the standard interfaces and object descriptions/UPnP actions are used, this will always be possible because the binding of the camera with a printer happens "magically" at execution time.

Patch IV. Web Services

Introduction Year	1998
Principle	Bypass the Web's presentation layer and provide an XML interface to servers' objects.
Patch to	Inadequacy of the Web as a computational infrastructure.
Standardization	OASIS, W3C, OGF.
Status	Still widely used, especially in their REST manifestation.
Related Techniques	ebXML, HP eServices, CORBA.

7.4   Service-Oriented Computing

At the turn of the century, industry was leading the effort from the technological side and producing new proposals very rapidly. Web Service Standards were soon covering interoperability, reliability, messaging, wiring, security, transactions, management, business process, quality of service, and more [112]. Researchers from academia soon perceived an opportunity for contributing. The Web Service technology, with its related publish-find-bind pattern, appeared to have a great potential for both system modeling and engineering. This led to the birth of a new computing sub-area, at times even considered an independent programming paradigm, *Service-Oriented Computing (SOC)*. Among the frontrunners of this movement stood Mike Papazoglou. One of his talents lies in the ability to translate technological trends into research questions and abstract frameworks. His 2003 paper together with Dimitri Georgakopoulus laid the foundations of SOC as an area, and it is still widely cited [97].

As the area of SOC is one to which I dedicated a good portion of my research efforts, I take the liberty here to fill the history of the Web with some personal experiences and recollections. In early 2002, I had just finished my PhD and met with Mike to discuss a possible collaboration in the context of a new appointment at the University of Trento in Italy. He illustrated the potential of the publish-find-bind pattern and of the related Web Service technologies. He then explained that it would be interesting to see how to take advantage of it in order to realize systems that can automatically compose services, that is, systems that, to achieve a business goal, can explore a service registry, find the needed components at run-time, and spontaneously create the business logic to achieve the original goal. A few months later, I went back to him and suggested three possible approaches: one based on Petri Nets, one on Statecharts, and one on Artificial Intelligence Planning. After several discussions, we decided to pursue the road of Artificial Intelligence Planning, as we felt it provided the right amount of flexibility and autonomy for the problem at hand. Mike recruited a brilliant PhD student, Alexander Lazovik, to work with us, and we started an exploration of service composition.

Our initial example was based on the organization of a trip on the Web [77]. To do so, one needs transportation, then an accommodation, and perhaps a ticket to some local musical event. These can be seen as separate object invocations exposed as WSDL services and accessible via SOAP. To create the travel, there are several possibilities. A straightforward approach is to resort to an off-line defined composition: identify the service providers, say

Air-Plane, ABC-Hotel, and FUN-EventTickets, and then write a program that invokes each one of them in a predefined order. A more flexible solution is that of identifying the types of services needed and the order in which these can be invoked, and then defer to run-time the actual finding of instances that comply with the composition. This is possible by using, for instance, the *Web Service Business Process Execution Language (BPEL)* that describes the logic for invoking services, enabling the late binding of service instances.

BPEL is an XML-based description of the flow of control and the logic of invocation of Web Services. It uses data types as described in WSDL, and uses WSDL also to refer to concrete Web Service instances. It is possible to use an UDDI registry to find the concrete implementation at run-time, again described in terms of WSDL. A composition can then be invoked as a single service itself, and again, WSDL acts as the interface language.

A BPEL document is composed of five sections: message flow, control flow, data flow, process, and orchestration exception handling. In describing the flows, it is possible to use structured-programming constructs such as if-then-elseif-else, while, and sequence. It is possible to describe *flows*, that is, parallel action executions (typically service invocations). BPEL has constructs for handling faults (similar to Java exceptions) and other more general event-handler constructs. It is a structured programming language whose basic object is a service-invocation/reply.

Using a simplified syntax, a BPEL process describing the travel composition could look something like the following:

```
<process name=''TravelProcess'' ... >
  <!--  Roles played by actual process
   participants at endpoints of an interaction -->
  <partnerLinks> find in UDDI
              use ABC-Hotel with role hotel-provider
                                    </partnerLinks >

  <!-- Data used by the process -->
  <variables> travel distance
            travel date
            price </ variables >

  <!-- Supports asynchronous interactions -->
  <correlationSets> ... </correlationSets>

  <!-- Activities that the process performs -->
   if travel distance >500km book flight from UDDI search
   book hotel from ABC-Hotel
  <!--Exception handling: Alternate execution path to deal with
      faulty situations -->
  <faultHandlers> handle exception </faultHandlers>

  <!--Code  that is executed when an action is ''undone'' -->
```

```
<compensationHandlers> get money back </compensationHandlers>

<!--Handling of concurrent events -->
<eventHandlers> send notification email </eventHandlers>
</process>
```

BPEL allows the description of compositions with a good degree of flexibility, adding structured commands for controlling the flow of execution, such as if-then-else constructs. It allows both fixed binding to services and run-time discovery, for instance by searching UDDI registries. A very powerful infrastructure for composition. But we wanted more.

7.5   A Personal Tale: Compose It Now!

Consider buying a Lego set. One gets a bag or box with many colorful pieces and a booklet with instructions. The pieces have standardized interfaces. The pegs are all the same size and match with the gaps of the pieces. Lego production standards mandate that the tolerance of these pegs and holes cannot exceed 0.08 mm. Lego bricks and other pieces can thus be composed, but how? The instructions guide the builder throughout the assembly process. Each step is indicated by a sequential number and involves the addition of a few pieces into components, finally resulting in full constructions. Sometimes the same component needs to be built two or more times, so the instruction will indicate this as "x2, x3, ..." signs. The instructions are a fixed composition with a sequence of operations, each one having few parallel actions and the possibility of fixed looping. The resulting composition is a fun toy to play with. Though, one of the cornerstones of Lego's success is the fact that one can potentially create any kind of composition. Kids love to assemble their own cars and castles. Artists like Nathan Sawaya create unique compositions such as human-size figures. Scientists enjoy building abstract computing machines in concrete forms, like the Turing machine built at CWI out of Lego pieces in 2012.

Moving from plastic to networked software, there are many similarities with Web Services. Lego bricks are much like individual services. Their peg-based interfaces define a compatible way of composing individual pieces, exactly like WSDL/SOAP allows one to bind atomic services. The instructions to assemble Lego constructions could easily be described in BPEL as a sequence of `flow` instructions with a `while` for any loop. And the developer can deviate from the instructions and write her own program to compose them.

My challenge in service composition has been that of describing the properties of the executing composition, minimizing the connections to actual services and their state. Using the Lego metaphor, say that one wants to build a castle, with four towers, and a drawbridge. The world is full of bricks, say potentially infinitely many. One can find the desired shaped one by digging with the hands in large piles of bricks, shuffling them around to expose the ones underneath. While one has an ideal castle in mind, other people can shuffle the bricks around and also pick up pieces that were necessary for the castle, forcing an adaptation in the original design due to the availability of pieces during assembly. What one desires is a system/robot that can transform any ideal design of a castle into an actual construction using the pieces that are available at construction time.

Such automatic Lego construction falls into what I define as the problem of *dynamic service composition*. More precisely, given a set of autonomous services described in a standard way, a *service composition* is an algorithm describing which service to execute when. The algorithm can be simple, such as a sequence of invocations or a Lego instruction booklet. But it can also be a very general description, considering many variations to achieve some composition goal. Artificial Intelligence Planning is a way of creating such dynamic and adaptable compositions.

Artificial Intelligence Planning is a branch of Artificial Intelligence concerned with the generation and execution of a set of actions to achieve some goal [55]. One provides a goal to the system, which takes into account the state of the world, also known as the initial state, and the description of the world in which it executes, the environment. The planner then provides a program for the realization of the goal, that is, the service composition. The program is given to an executor for actual realization—what in the service community is known as an *orchestrator*. Finally, the user provides a goal, a complex service composition request. The world is presented in terms of WSDL or other service description languages that can be located via some form of registries, such as UDDI.

In the early 2000s, several researchers proposed planning for Web interactions [70, 86, 87]. I was interested in a related problem: the challenge of Web Service composition, particularly, via planning. Moving to Trento also opened up the possibility to work with a research group that was well-known for its planning research. Mike and I illustrated the problem to them and suggested we use their existing planner to build the first prototype. I decided to translate the problem into a constraint satisfaction one, and our first design appeared in 2002 [4]. The collaboration didn't last long, though. From our perspective, we realized that the existing planner lacked in practice many of the advertised features. So we moved on, and built our own planners [54, 65, 78].

Our most recent result is the RuGCo planner [65]. There are a number of features that make it unique and especially useful for Web Service composition. The planner is built on the principle that the execution of a service invocation can fail or return values outside of the expected range, so-called byzantine behavior. It interleaves the planning phases with execution ones, where the obtained results are evaluated to decide how to continue the execution. It also accepts that results from service invocations are volatile and may change before the whole plan is executed, similar to someone taking a Lego piece away from a user wanting to construct something. Such uncertainty about service invocation can also be caused by other actors interfering with the plan execution. Using slightly more technical terms, it is a continual planner that is domain independent, solves a bounded planning problem, avoids grounding, and produces plans with parallel actions. I refer to it as being able to "Compose it now!" I say that to emphasize its ability to create compositions just in time and based on the execution environment of the moment of invocation. This means that the very same goal can result in different executions based on the starting condition and the execution environment. Flying or taking a train to a destination, when creating a travel package, will depend on the actual availability and prices of flights on specific dates. In fact, our proposed approach is so flexible in adapting to uncertain and concurrent environments, that we have also used it for bringing smartness to homes equipped with wireless sensors and actuators, going beyond the Web composition case [66].

~

Service composition might very well go in the direction of Web objects as viewed by Alan Kay. The Web focuses on the presentation layer and the hyper-mediality, while Kay advocates a Web of objects for which browsers are object loaders. Web Services disregard the presentation layer and offer explicitly the functionality behind the service. The XML verbose syntax provides a form of unified interfaces accessible to all. Web Services lack explicit semantics that can allow for a well-designed worldwide interface; actually, they lack any form of semantics at all. They are just standardized interfaces, object binders, and policy descriptors. Though, at least they are about distributed execution. In this scenario, service composition is the technique that can provide added value to the distributed services, especially if the service composition can occur on demand and is adaptive to varying contextual circumstances. Approaches to service composition are my small, though passionate, contribution to the field.

It is far from being widely used or commercialized. However, as it is the case with many techniques based on Artificial Intelligence, it may provide a good support for humans in the long-term, just like personal digital assistants, home robots, and self-driving cars. To date, automatic composition is still considered a major challenge in the field of Service-Oriented Computing [25].

7.6   The Patch

The first three patches introduced in Chap. 6 serve the purpose of bringing dynamic content to Web pages by allowing computation to take place on the client side together with the interpretation of the HTML tags. Web Services take it one step further by decoupling the computation even from the HTML and simply offering the server's resources via an XML interface. Before their introduction, developers wishing to retrieve something on a Web page as a service, had to write an HTML interpreter and mimic human interaction with the website. To incorporate, say, a train schedule on a Web page, one writes a piece of code that connects to the Web page of the train company, and then one scraps data from the results to add it to the new system. If the original webserver changes its layout, or starts restricting the number of accesses per client, such an approach breaks.

With Web Services, one can ignore the presentation layer and the tags and ask directly for the service as a set of direct object invocations embedded in XML. No presentation layer is needed, and the object invocation is described by its IDL interface, and hopefully some additional technical and business information on its use is included. eBay was one of the early players to jump into the field. By the end of the century, its growing popularity, and economic potential for its customers, also meant that it was experiencing a heavy load of software systems accessing the website for the automatic processing of items to auction. Think of selling a whole collection of stamps. It would take days, if not months, to go through the Web pages of eBay and place the stamps for sale one by one. A more scalable and efficient solution is to write a program that accesses your own database with all the stamps you have and automatically uploads them to the auction site. On November 20, 2000, eBay launched its Developers Program and the initial set of *Application Programmable Interfaces (APIs)*, soon followed by a Web Service version of them. In this way, eBay went beyond being merely a place for collectors and people wanting to resell their second-hand stuff and became an eCommerce platform with a worldwide audience. Amazon followed with its Web Service platform in July of 2002, and all major Web players soon would accompany their websites with Web Service-based access.

Web Services patch the Web by providing object to object direct invocations that are independent of any hypertextual presentation. The coupling between objects can be delayed as late as execution time, allowing for loose-coupling and late-binding. It is such a powerful pattern that it deserved its own brand of computing, the Service-Oriented Computing approach to system engineering. The concept of abstracting object to object interactions as services has been so widely accepted ever since that people have started incorporating human instances into the electronic ones and have been talking about the new field of *Service Science* [106].

7.7   Who's Serving?

In the eighteenth century, Wolfgang von Kempelen toured Europe and the Americas with a unique machine. It was capable of playing chess on its own and frequently winning. The machine was the size of a desk-like cabinet. Some complicated mechanics were visible on one side, while a wooden mannequin dressed as a Turk would move the chess pieces on top of it. The machine was exhibited and played for various nobles and kings across the world, astonishing the public. Interestingly, the actual intelligence of the machine came from a human who was hosted inside it. The human could control the Turk's movements while having a replicated view of the chess board on top of the desk. Various chess experts have donated their skills to the mechanical Turk over the years, invariably attracting attention to such an engineering wonder. In reality, the world would have to wait another two and a half centuries before witnessing automata becoming world champions. In 1997, IBM's Deep Blue realization won in a series of games over Gary Kasparov and became the world's best chess player [32].

The legacy of that machine has given the name to a notable use of Web Services today. Amazon's Mechanical Turk, launched in 2005 and created from an idea of the brilliant developer and entrepreneur Venky Harinarayan, is based on the concept that people can offer services to be consumed by programs. WSDL descriptions of tasks are offered on its platform, and people can accept them and perform the service, returning a message, again, following the WSDL specification [82]. This is especially useful for tasks that are hard to solve with a software program, e.g., providing input to surveys, identifying what is in a digital image, correlating user profiles from Facebook with others from LinkedIn, and so on. With something like Amazon Turk, service implementations are so decoupled from their invokers as to even be performed by human beings, not using any programming language at all, just natural intelligence.

A somewhat similar inspiration is what led Active Endpoints, Adobe, BEA, IBM, Oracle, and SAP to publish the `BPEL4People` and `WS-HumanTask` specifications in 2007. These allow the integration of human activities into service compositions, so that a software process activity can be followed by a manual operation by a human participating in the service composition.

7.8 XML Web Services Versus the REST

Having contributed to the HTTP 1.1 standard during his studies, Roy Fielding defended his PhD thesis in 2000 at the University of California, Irvine, on network-based software architectures [48]. He defines a component as an "abstract unit of software instructions and internal state that provides a transformation of data via its interface" and proposes an architectural style derived from his Web experience. He considers it necessary that the servers of a networked application be forced to satisfy six general constraints in order to be scalable, simple, modifiable, and reliable. The six constraints are named: client-server, stateless, cacheable, layered, code on demand, and uniform interface. He called this style *Representational State Transfer (REST)*, putting emphasis on the fact that the operations on the server are stateless and that interactions between clients and servers must include the state of the session as part of their request and reply.

REST naturally relies on the stateless HTTP protocol (Sect. 4.2), while putting no requirements on the content to be transported. It is a stateless alternative to SOAP/WSDL-based Web Services. Let's name these *XML Web Services* and the REST-based alternative *REST Web Services*. REST filled the gap of having a simple and workable solution, overcoming the complexity and overheads necessary for Web Service-based interoperation. The XML Web Service approach works well for discrete business invocations, while it has no good provision for multimedia or streaming applications.

The debate between XML Web Services versus the REST also broke into the academic community. About 10 years ago, it was common to have corridor discussions on the topic during the major SOC conferences, with the groups equally divided into those against and those in favor of RESTful services. In 2007, the first paper on REST appeared at a workshop of the International Conference on Service-Oriented Computing (ICSOC), and another one was presented in the main conference of IEEE International Conference on Web Services (ICWS) of 2008. By 2009, REST had its own track at ICWS.

Relying on all operations of the HTTP protocol, REST is indeed an efficient way of realizing Web interoperability, but it still requires quite some negotiation between the developers of the client and the server to agree on what is the content of the message. Nevertheless, it has been gaining popularity for its performance. For example, since 2016 the eBay API are based on JSON REST specifications.

REST deviates further away than XML Web Services from Kay's desire for clean semantics for distributed objects, though it does address a performance issue which is strongly related to the use of XML. XML is heavy both in verbosity and the need of processing resources. About the same time that REST was proposed, hardware vendors—hardware!—started to market XML routers. It started with DataPower (later acquired by IBM) and Vordel in 1999, Sarvega in 2000, and others followed. The idea was to have routers processing and routing XML messages directly without calling applications to inspect their content, mimicking the Internet routing, but using XML content to decide the destination, rather than an IP address [73]. Since the use for XML-based message-oriented systems, like Web Service middleware, was the prominent one, sometimes such devices were called Service-Oriented Architecture Routers. Today, the increased performance of computers and consequent speed of XML processing have made these XML appliances uninteresting. The success of REST may also have helped phase the hardware XML routers out.

7.9 Vaporizing Services

Web Service-based protocols have been widely used beyond the Web, most notably, for information system integration. The *Enterprise Service Bus (ESB)* is an architectural model for realizing such integration of systems. David Chappell identified a set of ESB patterns and proposed a graphic notation for designing such ESB, though no specific standard followed [37]. ESB leverages on publish-subscribe architectures, asynchronous publish-subscribe messaging, and XML. Their strong selling point is the ability to put together very heterogenous systems, typically including very old legacy components. They scale reasonably well, though they pay the price of heavy XML messaging. Most large vendors have a solution in the area, though some are starting to phase them out. IBM announced that its WebSphere Enterprise Service Bus will reach the end of its life in 2018.

Another crucial technology in the Web Service scenario is UDDI, introduced in Sect. 7.3. In the early days, the vision was that of having a global UDDI registry for the whole Web. Similar to the Domain Name System (DNS) for resolving names applied for the identification of all Internet-available Web Services. The global declination of UDDI, known as *Universal Business Registry (UBR)*, was an initiative of IBM, Microsoft, and SAP. Though it proved to be technically feasible, it never took off and was officially shut down with a short communication from the standardization body OASIS. "With the approval of UDDI v3.02 as an OASIS Standard in 2005, and the momentum UDDI has achieved in market adoption, IBM, Microsoft and SAP have evaluated the status of the UDDI Business Registry and determined that the goals for the project have been achieved. Given this, the UDDI Business Registry will be discontinued as of 12 January 2006."

An important trend that has had meaningful impact on the technological landscape of today, and to which Web Services have contributed to, is that of *Cloud Computing* [59]. Web Services inspired the realization that operations could be available via a network as a service. But why just services for remote object invocation? Via the network, one could offer the hardware platform and its storage capability *as a service;* or databases, development tools, and Web servers; or as entire applications, word processors, and emails. From the hardware to the application, the offer of everything as a service took multiple names, each representing the type of offer: *Infrastructure as a Service (IaaS)*, *Platform as a Service (PaaS)*, and *Software as a Service (SaaS)*. Service-Oriented Architectures tend to fall into the latter category. With the movement towards everything as a service, computing-related resources thus lose the nature of a commodity and become an utility.

Amazon has been a frontrunner in understanding the value of such an approach for its business and the potential market size based on the intuition of its current CTO, Werner Vogels. The Dutch researcher got his PhD from the Vrije Universiteit Amsterdam after spending years as a researcher at Cornell, investigating scalable and reliable enterprise information systems. Vogels joined Amazon soon after and became the CTO in early 2005. He noticed two important things at Amazon. The first one was the popularity of their Web Services' API with developers, who had formed a very active user community. The second was an important under-utilization of computing infrastructure by the companies owning the infrastructure. He writes, "From experience we knew that the cost of maintaining a reliable, scalable infrastructure in a traditional multi-datacenter model could be as high as 70%, both in time and effort. [...] We were also keenly aware that compute utilization in most cases, enterprise as well as startups, is dramatically low (less than 20% and often even lower than 10%) and is often subject to significant periodicity" [116]. In 2006, *Amazon Web Services (AWS)* were officially launched.[2]

A classic example of computing as a utility is that of a small company called Animoto. Their original product was online software for the creation of videos out of image collections, adding value to customer's images, and requiring a fair deal of processing power to run. In the startup phase of the company, they were using their own hardware for the processing of images into videos, and fielding a few hundreds users per day. Each user request for a video required a dedicated process running on the GPU of their computers. When in 2008 they became a fast hit on Facebook, their user application attracted 750,000 new users in just three days, with a peak of 25,000 in one hour. Animoto's hardware infrastructure would have needed to be upgraded 100 times and would have taken several months to set up. Luckily they had migrated to the Amazon Cloud a few months earlier, and scaling to meet the sudden burst in demand was not a problem [49].

Amazon was the first big player to enter the cloud arena with its AWS, launching the *Simple Storage Service (S3)*, the *Simple Queue Service (SQS)*, and the *Elastic Compute Cloud (EC2)* in 2006. AWS are a form of offering at the infrastructure level, accessible with SOAP XML messages and using the REST architectural style. Some companies today use AWS as their sole infrastructure. Netflix relies entirely on AWS, as do the Kempinski Hotels. Dropbox was also entirely AWS-based until they reached a size to justify the building of their own infrastructure. In 2016, AWS provided for about 10% of Amazon's net income (12 billion US dollars out of 135 billions) and, more interestingly, a staggering 75% of its operating income. One could argue that the "book company" Amazon makes most of their profits by selling computational resources.

In 2014, I attended a conference on Information Systems. Looking at the program, I was intrigued by the list of excellent keynote speakers. One of them would talk about "Fog Computing." Expecting a hilarious exposition on how cloud computing had been hyped, I eagerly attended the keynote. To my surprise, and somewhat disappointment, the talk was a serious and technically informed discussion of a new trend in cloud computing, where clients store data and use local networking facilities to get the functionalities they need, reducing the direct services from the clouds. So the vapor-services of the clouds go down, closer to the surface of the earth where the devices live, turning into fog. A reminder of the fat client model. Though the fat is not all

---

[2]The story of the origin of AWS is often presented as Amazon wanting to sell its own overcapacity, which is especially considerable outside of the Christmas holidays period. On several occasions, Vogels has labelled such an account as a myth.

on one client, but is rather shared among the various components which are physically close to each other [22]. One year after that conference, Cisco, Intel, Microsoft, and other partners formed the *OpenFog* consortium to promote the concept of Fog Computing and consider steps towards the standardization of protocols.

Having personal devices and computers with strong computational and networking capabilities for sure helps propel the trend of making the client/user side "fatter," though there is more. The increasing availability of "things" being connected to the Internet and accessible both programmatically and by users via dedicated apps, the so-called *Internet of Things (IoT)* trend, also calls for architectures where important processing steps happen close to the client, before interaction with the clouds. The amount of data generated by these devices is such that transmitting all of it raw for centralized processing in the cloud is ineffective, if even feasible at all. New trends are emerging where the computation happens at the periphery of the network. This trend, known as *Edge Computing*, puts the emphasis less on the service aspects and more on where the data processing takes place [18, 85]. Other similar flavors and names for closely related ideas are Dew Computing, Grid/Mesh Computing, and Cloudlet.

Figure 7.5 illustrates the trend from the client-server model towards the current popular approaches. If the Web and its Web Service patch have supported a model for highly decoupled systems, the cloud has vaporized the services even further and put them behind thick clouds. Services become omnipresent and include storage, computations, and application suites. From

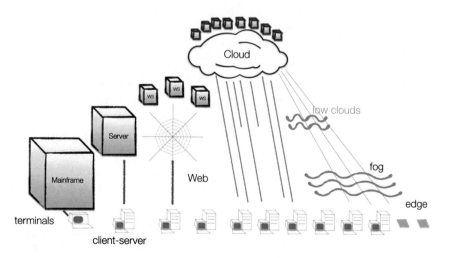

Fig. 7.5 Architecture evolution

clouds, the vaporized services redescend towards the client in the form of Fog Computing. This is facilitated by the increasing computational power of the (fat) clients and by the advanced networking features of present times, pushing to model it further as Edge Computing.

8

The Unexploited Patch

ΟΝΤΟΛΟΓΙΑ for Everything

"Now! That *should clear up a few things around here!"*
Gary Larson

The very first system built by Tim Berners-Lee to store information about people, projects, and systems at CERN used qualified links (Chap. 3). Entities were related by terms such as `made`, `includes`, `uses`, and `describes`. That original idea of labelled links, though, disappeared from HTML and the first incarnations of the Web. About 10 years later, Tim Berners-Lee was ready to propose their reintroduction, and not only of a few specific terms, but rather an entire framework and set of protocols for the specification of annotations relating to Web content. The proposal supported the formal expression of the meaning of textual resources and the relation among concepts expressed in the text. The framework's aim was to make the semantics of data and links in Web pages explicit and unambiguously specified.

"I have a dream for the Web…and it has two parts. In the first part, the Web becomes a much more powerful means for collaboration between people. I have always imagined the information space as something to which everyone has immediate and intuitive access, and not just to browse, but to create. […] In the second part of the dream, collaborations extend to computers. Machines become capable of analyzing all the data on the Web—the content, links, and transactions between people and computers. A 'Semantic Web,' which should make this possible, has yet to emerge, but when it does, the day-to-day mechanisms of trade, bureaucracy and our daily lives will be

© Springer International Publishing AG, part of Springer Nature 2018
M. Aiello, *The Web Was Done by Amateurs*,
https://doi.org/10.1007/978-3-319-90008-7_8

handled by machines talking to machines." So writes Tim Berners-Lee in his 1999 book [19]. A *Scientific American* paper, published in 2001, follows up with the goal of reaching out to a broader audience of the scientific community [20].

8.1   The Semantic Gap

There is a semantic gap between a string in an HTML document and the concept it represents. The italic string *<i>Logo</i>* placed in an HTML document may refer to the concept of the functional programming language Logo or the concept of an icon representing a company, product, university, or other organizations. HTML documents do not provide means to fill the semantic gap occurring between a word specified by its letters and its meaning. The goal of the *Semantic Web*, as proposed by Tim Berners-Lee, is to establish a set of technologies to fill that gap and to do it in a way compatible with the existing and successful hypertextual Web.

To achieve such a goal, two major ingredients are required. First, one needs a system to specify meanings, to express concepts, and to define relations among them. One needs an ontological foundation. Second, one needs a vocabulary that allows the association of terms with their intended meaning. The Semantic Web has provisions for both.

$$\sim$$

Ontology refers to the study of the nature of things and their classification. Being a subfield of philosophy, the term is typically used in the singular form. In computer science, the term was extended to refer to any formal representation of concepts employed by a system to operate [6]. Under this definition, it is thus common to consider the existence of many ontologies: one for every running system, or even one for every instance of a running system.

Considering again Universal Plug and Play (Sect. 7.3), we notice how devices are described as a set of features, services, and icons. These are presented using the XML language. The following is an excerpt from the UPnP XML device specification.

```
<device>
    <friendlyName>___</friendlyName>
    <manufacturer>___</manufacturer>
    [...]
    <serviceList>
      <service>
         <serviceType>___</serviceType>
         <serviceId>___</serviceId>
```

```
      [...]
    </service>
  </serviceList>
  <deviceList>___</deviceList>
  <iconList>
      <icon>___</icon>
  </iconList>
</device>
```

We can regard such an XML description as a very simple form of ontology without constraints beyond the syntactic ones. By direct inspection, we understand that there is a concept of a device. The device has a set of properties, like a name, a manufacturer, but also a list of services that can be invoked and a list of icons associated with it. By using the nesting of XML tags, we obtain a hierarchical description of the domain of UPnP devices.

Semantic Web techniques are a more refined form of ontological descriptions that suit the Web domain. It is not one protocol, but rather a set of them. The most basic and widespread one is the *Resource Description Framework (RDF)*. It is a data modeling language based on statements providing binary relationships among entities, plus a set of ontological definitions (called *RDF Schemas*). RDF's and RDFS' first versions were released by the W3C consortium in 1998 and 1999, respectively. Final recommendations were published in 2004, followed in 2014 by a major update just for RDF with Version 1.1.

The building blocks of RDF are resources, properties, and statements. Resources are items to which one associates a meaning, say, the book *Moby Dick* or the writer Herman Melville. Properties describe the relationships among resources, such as the fact that authors write books. Statements connect resources as subject–predicate–object triples. In our example, the statement about the book becomes a binary predicate: *WriterOf(Melville, Moby Dick)*. RDF can be represented in many ways. XML is a possible syntax for it, though other graphical representations are equally valid. We show the book example using a graphical notation in Fig. 8.1. With RDF we are able to express binary predicates. To provide a more comprehensive ontological view, it is useful to consider the higher level of abstraction and to move from instances to concepts representing them collectively. In this way, we can also constrain and define how instances can be related together by RDF statements. Figure 8.2 shows the RDF example of the book put in relation with a possible originating RDFS. Melville is an instance of the class "person," while the novel *Moby Dick* is an instance of the class "book." This fact is expressed by rdf:type properties. At the RDFS level, we define the concept of a person to be included in the concept of mammals with the rdfs:SubClassOf property, and similarly for the class of a "whale." RDFS can also qualify how an RDF relation is related

Fig. 8.1 An RDF statement

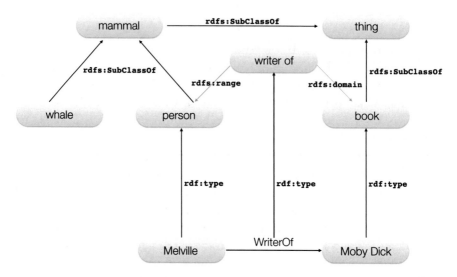

Fig. 8.2 An RDF schema with instances

to entities; in fact, the property of being the "writer of" ranges over "person," having as the domain of its association the class of a "book." From the example, one should have an impression of the power of RDFS. It allows one to define an ontology of classes and properties, with a simple construct to create instances.

RDF is a nifty combination of being a simple modeling language while also functioning as an expressive ontological language. It has provisions for allowing one to write statements about statements, known as *reification*, which is a quite powerful construct. It is, for instance, possible to create self-referring loops. On the other hand, it is limited to binary relations, which can make the expression of some concepts quite cumbersome. Say that one wants to express the concept of a book launch. That involves a multi-valued relation, something like book_launch(author, book, publisher, date). RDF forces the user to express this as a set of binary relations—launch(event, book), writer(event, author), printed(event, publisher), time(event, date)—a process that is both unnatural and error prone. Furthermore, RDF does not allow local scoping of properties, so one cannot declare range restrictions that apply to only some specific subclasses. One cannot express cardinality restrictions, such as forcing a relation to be instantiated only a finite number of times, e.g., a whale having only one blowhole. It is also not possible to state that two classes are disjoint, that is, that individuals can be members of either class, but not of both. More generally, it is not possible to use any form of set operators and combinations of quantification on classes, such as union, intersection, and complement.

The continuous research effort on ontologies combined with some of the limitations of RDF brought about a number of proposals following the initial RDFS W3C recommendations. In 1999, James Hendler from DARPA started a research program on machine-readable representation for the Web, having Tim Berners-Lee as one of the principal investigators. The program resulted, among other things, in the proposal of the *DARPA Machine Markup Language (DAML)*. Based on RDF and its XML syntax, it was a first extension towards the Semantic Web vision. The research program soon became synergic to the homologous European one, financed by the European Commission, and in March 2001 it was decided that the European effort, called *Ontology Inference Layer (OIL)*, and DAML should merge. The synergic proposal coming from DAML+OIL was intended to be a thin layer above RDFS with a full specified semantics. The joint effort produced a family of languages called *Ontology Web Languages (OWL)*, which became a formal W3C recommendation in early 2004.

The language OWL is based on RDF; it is typically represented using XML or graphical notations. There are three major OWL sublanguages. *OWL Full* is the most expressive one, allowing multivalued relations and classes about classes' statements. Furthermore, in OWL Full an ontology can redefine the meaning of its own vocabulary. Given the expressive power of OWL Full and its close relation to first-order logic, deciding whether a statement is derivable or not is, in general, not possible (by reduction to the 1930s result of Gödel); therefore, decidable fragments of OWL Full have been proposed. OWL Description Logic or *OWL DL* solves this problem, being the largest fragment of OWL to be amenable to decidable reasoning procedures. It is based on description logics that are known to be in a decidable fragment of first-order logic.

OWL DL limits the use and combination of some constructs. For instance, number restrictions cannot be used for transitive relations. *OWL Lite* excludes enumerated classes, disjointness statements, and arbitrary cardinality, making it very similar to RDF without reification, though still allowing the possibility of having multivalued relations. It is easy to show that there is a strict inclusion, in terms of expressive power: OWL Lite $\subset$ OWL DL $\subset$ OWL Full.

8.2   Subsumptions Subsumed by Subsumptions

The Semantic Web introduces protocols and techniques to define ontologies regarding specific domains. The benefit of having such an infrastructure resides in the possibility to perform reasoning automatically. Possible reasoning tasks include:

Class membership.   Checking whether an individual is a member of a given class. E.g., assessing that Moby Dick is an instance of the class of sperm whales.

Individual retrieval.   Getting all members of a given class. E.g., getting a list of all the hundreds of thousands of instances of sperm whales in the world.

Individual classification and realization.   Identifying the most specific class which an individual belongs to or, more generally, identifying all classes to which an individual belongs. E.g., Moby Dick belongs to the class of sperm whales.

Class satisfiability.   Checking whether the definition of a class allows for it to contain at least one member. E.g., the class of ocean animals that feeds milk to their calves has instances in the form of whales and dolphins, while the class of egg-laying biped mammals is a class that no individual can satisfy.

Class equivalence.   Checking whether two or more classes are equivalent to each other, though defined by different names or sets of properties. This includes checking the transitivity of the equivalence relation among classes. E.g., using the official Latin names of the animal families to assess that the class of whales is equivalent to that of cetacea minus delphinidae.

Consistency.   Checking that a set of statements are not contradicting each other. For instance, stating that whales and people are disjoint classes and stating that Moby Dick is a member of both classes is an inconsistent statement.

Subsumption.   Determining the hierarchical relation among classes based on the concept of "being a subcase of." E.g., the fact that Moby Dick is a whale automatically means that Moby Dick is also a mammal and in turn a living being, given that whales are subclasses of mammals and mammals are subclasses of living beings.[1]

---

[1]The subsumption relation is a partial, reflexive, transitive, and antisymmetric relation. In plain terms, it means that if people are mammals, mammals are animals, and aliens exist, then people are animals

All these forms of reasoning are very useful for the understanding and retrieval of information. If one is looking for a car to hire, an automatic system could reason by subsumption and conclude that a car is actually a transportation means, and it could then find a disjoint subclass—for instance, the class of railway-based systems and a specific train company—by means of individual retrieval. The Semantic Web can thus aid by providing a semantic layer in between the existing textual-based Web and the user interacting with it.

The foundations of the reasoning mechanisms which the Semantic Web relies on are the solid result of long scientific investigation. At the origin there was the desire to represent knowledge and data on the basis of logical, graphical, and cognitive-based specifications. From the semantic networks proposed in the 1970s, investigations of terminological systems spun off in the 1980s, till a community gathered around the area of *description logics* with an annual series of events, starting from a 1991 Dagstuhl seminar [8, 122].

Description logics are formal languages for which the basic entities are individuals and concepts. It is possible to employ usual boolean connectors among these and to express relations such as one concept being a subclass of another one. Description logics are a whole family of languages differentiated by what can be expressed about the relation among concepts and what operations can be done on the classes. What has made them very popular is their elegant approach to data modeling and the computational properties that most of them enjoy. In fact, it has been proven that most of these logics are decidable unlike first-order languages, of which they are a strict subset. Decidability has been proven in several ways, for instance, by Maurizio Lenzerini and his colleagues by relating description logic to modal logics and, more generally, to logical languages that belong to the so-called "two-variable guarded fragment" of first-order logic [44].

OWL DL derives the description language $\mathcal{SHOIN}^{\mathcal{D}}$, i.e., the attributive description logic with transitive roles, role hierarchy, nominals, inverse proper-ties, cardinality restrictions, and datatype properties. OWL Lite is based on the language $\mathcal{SHIF}^{\mathcal{D}}$, i.e., the attributive description logic with transitive roles, role hierarchy, functional properties, and datatype properties. Both languages are decidable, being in the guarded fragment of first-order logic. In simpler terms, the OWL languages derive from solid theoretical foundations, making sure that all statements that can be expressed can be managed by an automatic reasoner that performs inference over their statements.

(transitivity), people are people (reflexivity), not all animals are people (antisymmetry), and nothing can be said of the relation between people and aliens (partiality). Therefore, the subsumption relation is also subsumed by other relations, including itself, hence the title of this section.

Patch V. Semantic Web

Introduction Year	1999
Principle	Add ontological annotations to terms and links on Web pages.
Patch to	Lack of well-founded and structured information on the Web.
Standardization	W3C
Status	Not successful as a Web patch. Successfully used in confined projects, most often outside the Web context.
Related Techniques	No closely related Web technique.

8.3   The Patch

The Semantic Web is such a radical addition to the original 1989 Web that it might better fit the category of a major redesign, rather than that of a patch. On the other hand, given that it was proposed after the Web and it was designed to be compatible with it, I still classify it as a patch. I actually consider it the Mother of All Patches.

Coming from the very same inventor of the Web, the Semantic Web had a completely different origin and destiny. It comes from well-researched theories. It is based on provable properties, such as computational complexity of reasoning, decidability of its procedures, and a formal semantic foundation. It is absolutely not the product of amateurs, but rather a concerted effort of the best minds involved in the field of knowledge representation and databases.

The Semantic Web is intriguing and appealing to the scientist as it possesses a clean, logical approach to the systematization of representations and, in turn, of aspects of the world. It has that purity in creating scientific taxonomies that has revolutionized biology thanks to the proposal of Linneus. It is that systematic approach that scientists and engineers fall in love with. Even though, the Semantic Web is based on years of fundamental research in computer science, it still failed to patch the Web.

Considering the adoption rate of Semantic Web and its actual use on the Web, one can only remark that it never really took off on a global scale. A few million websites have RDF annotations. The number is not as big as it might at first appear, considering that there are billions of websites available at the moment. Furthermore, the number of tools and search engines actually taking advantage of these annotations is unknown and believed to be very limited.

Such a lack of adoption, does not mean that Semantic Web technology is useless. On the contrary, there have been plenty of successful reports on its use in industry; for example, in the medical domain, diagnosis systems use OWL to model their data. Semantic Web technologies have also been reported as part of IBM Watson, the system that in 2011 beat the human champions at the television game show Jeopardy!

Before we discuss why the Semantic Web is a patch that has experienced little practical success, let me provide a personal anecdote. A few years back, I was in Brussels with a couple of colleagues to negotiate the terms of a European project we had just been granted. During that meeting, the conversation with the European Union Project Officer [PO] went more or less like this:

[PO:] "Regarding expenses, we do pay on the basis of receipts and evidence. We ask for a controller if the total budget of a unit is above 375.000 euros, and more or less everything is covered."

[Us:] "Anything we should be careful with?"

[PO:] "Not really, but don't exaggerate. We recently had two cases that caused controversy."

[Us:] "Like what?"

[PO:] "Once a consortium rented a private jet to go to a project meeting, while another time another consortium held its gathering in a villa, on the Côte d'Azur…during the Cannes film festival."

[Us:] "We see. No worries, we don't plan anything like that."

I do not know about the villa, but the private jet was a Semantic Web project. It was a sign of the times. The Semantic Web was a young and very promising technology. The European Union felt the Web to be a pride of its research system, with its CERN origins and a British father, and at the same time saw the opportunity to consolidate the leadership by promoting and financing innovation in what looked like the natural major innovation of the original Web, the movement towards the Semantic Web. To make sure that innovation was not hindered by lack of funding, it poured great amounts of money into Semantic Web-related projects, dedicating entire calls to the theme. After the merger of the DARPA working group on DAML with the European OIL one, more and more targeted calls were supporting Semantic Web research. This was true in both the Sixth and the Seventh European Frameworks (2002–2013). In the first two calls of FP6, 137 million euros went to Semantic Web projects, with an additional 125 assigned in Call 4. Accounting for the exact amount of money that went to Semantic Web research in the last decade is not easy, because of both the difficulties in digging information from the website of the EU, and the difficulty to precisely discern between projects predominantly about the Semantic Web from those having only some elements of it. Let us just say that it is likely that a currency amount close to a billion has gone to Semantic Web research, providing a platform for developing excellent research results, many investigations into industrial applications, and also a flight or two on a private jet. The Web, though, has evolved in different directions.

$\sim$

The Semantic Web is a patch to the Web as it addresses the uplifting of the hypertextual system to a system of concepts, to words with well-defined meaning. It moves from textual pages towards semantically specified descriptions over which one can formally reason. However, it has failed to become a useful patch. The reason for such a failure can be sought in the alternative approaches to fill that semantic gap introduced in Sect. 8.1.

The alternative approach to extract meaning from pages, or better said, for improving the quality of information retrieval, is a statistical one. The one followed by modern search engines such as Google. The reasoning behind the statistical approach is this: rather than defining semantics and expecting them to be provided together with textual and multimedia content, why not try to extract meaning automatically? To be able to do so, one needs close to infinite amounts of data so that the semantic extraction process can become precise enough and the classification of a given page or text can be done based on a sufficiently large set of examples.

The success of the Web itself has provided huge amounts of data, which is in turn necessary for a statistic approach to be successful. The largest source of *Big Data* known, the Web, has so many instances of the word whale in so many different contexts that it is possible to interpret its use within any available Web page with reasonably high likelihood. So why bother to write an ontology and an RDF statement about it?

There is more. Using ontologies and defining what the meaning of a page is can be much more easily exploited by malicious users. In reality, users read the text on HTML pages as it is. On the other hand, the user is not going to read or inspect the ontological definition or the RDF statements. This means that a malicious provider can present a page about illegal or immoral transactions as a candid one about water mammals. Our experience with spam email and links that bring us to undesired corners of the Web should provide evidence for the actual risk that we run of falling victim to Web Dragons [120].

There is a third and mostly unexplored approach to filling the semantic gap. It is that hinted by Kay in his interview: to conceive of a Web made of well-defined executing objects, and to consider Web navigation as the composing of distributed objects in mobile operating systems, a modern form of browser. Admittedly, providing object specification will be more cumbersome for the end-user than using an editor to create HTML content. However, the success of HyperCard in the late 1980s, shows that non-programmers can, and are willing to, delve into computing ideas, if provided with the right tools and perceiving some form of utility. HyperCard had the merit of attracting tens of thousands of people to hypertextual programmable objects, most likely without most of them even being aware of it.

If the Semantic Web is the foundation of Tim Berners-Lee's vision for the Web and RDF and OWL are its incarnations, we might consider Kay's vision as having Obliq as a possible foundation for it. Obliq is a simple, distributed, object-oriented programming language that is lexically scoped [33]. In Obliq, objects can migrate from one node to another on the network, and their behavior is retained while changing location. Technically, the free identifiers are bound to their original locations, independently of the new location in the network topology. Similarly to Kay's SmallTalk, Obliq objects are just collections of named fields, but they do not have a hierarchical system of objects. A browser that supports Oblets, that is Obliq distributed containers, has been developed and is, to the best of my knowledge, the closest incarnation to Kay's vision of the browser as a loader of distributed objects [28].

Part IV

System Engineering

9

The Self-Organizing Web
One Web, an Infinity of Spiders

I don't need Google. My wife knows everything.
Anonymous

Asking Google about the weather forecast for tomorrow, the date of birth of a novelist, the number of words in Moby Dick, or what's playing at a nearby cinema has become common practice. The precision of the results is no longer a source of wonder, even though it mostly likely should be, given the refined techniques and body of information behind search engines. Who has provided all the information to Google so that it can be summarized, displayed, and easily accessed?

It is a collective and mostly spontaneous effort. Organizations reach a wide audience by publishing information relating to their business on their websites, people with specific interests often passionately write about them and love to share knowledge, and services offered by companies are provided on the Web as well as through other means. What is fascinating is the involvement of millions of individuals who provide data for the pleasure of sharing information about their lives and their passions. Currently, the Web has over one billion websites, more than 300 million people are active on Twitter (providing an average of 500 million tweets per day), an estimated 150 million blogs are accessible, and most organizations, if not all, have a Web presence.

No centralized control is enforced on such data generation and no direct incentives are provided—though a market for advertising and other forms of remuneration is very well developed and opulent—so there is something else that motivates people to contribute Web pages, links, and services to the Web.

© Springer International Publishing AG, part of Springer Nature 2018
M. Aiello, *The Web Was Done by Amateurs*,
https://doi.org/10.1007/978-3-319-90008-7_9

The spirit is very similar to the original contributions that saw the birth of the Web and its success. People saw a new technology and opportunity. Using it was easy and open. Tim Berners-Lee was actively supporting the use of the technologies he invented. A unique combination of factors created the Web.

In the following, we consider how such decentralized and self-organized contribution to the content of the Web and to its technologies has catered to its success. A number of properties of the Web have emerged spontaneously from the various independent efforts of individuals globally distributed, such as the shape of the Web and its relative compactness in terms of link paths.

9.1   The Size and Shape of the Web

The first Web page was Tim Berners-Lee's page at CERN. It went live on August 6, 1991. By the end of the same year, Stanford's SLAC pages went online. The year 1992 saw five more websites appear. These were tied to the following organizations: Nikhef, NCSA, Fermilab, SunSite, and Ohio State University. From there on, the growth has literally been exponential, as shown on the left of Fig. 9.1, while the right of the figure zooms into the data for the first years and first decade of the Web.[1] At the time of writing, we are approaching the 1.2 billion Web pages landmark. In counting the number of websites in the world, there is an important remark to make. For 1991 and 1992, one can come up with a precise and detailed account. This can go on for a couple of years further, but then it becomes impossible to exhaustively and precisely list all reachable websites. It is not a mere issue of size, as in too many to count, but rather the fact that websites appear and go without any centralized registration and control. Rather than a precise count, from 1994 on, people started making estimations of the size of the Web. Let us investigate how one can go about computing these values.

To "count" the number of websites, one takes advantage of software which navigates the Web automatically, known as a *crawler* or a *spider*. The crawler takes a number of seeds, that is, starting pages, and then follows the links that it finds on the pages. Logging and expanding all found links, it "crawls" around the Web. If the Web were a strongly connected graph, it would be possible to visit all pages and come up with a precise count of websites and pages. But this is far from true for the Web. So the quality of the exploration is a function

---

[1]NetCraft and Internet Live Stats; retrieved from: http://www.internetlivestats.com/total-number-of-websites/.

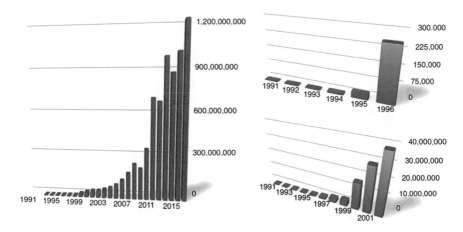

Fig. 9.1 Web growth since its birth

of the quality and quantity of the initial seeds. Furthermore, the number of websites can be defined in various ways based on the hosts, the URLs, and other identifiers tied to pages. The data used in Fig. 9.1 is based on the number of hostnames connected to sites that respond to the crawler, including parked pages—that is, domains registered that do not yet offer content.

In 1993, Matthew Gray, a physics student of MIT, wrote one of the first crawlers, the `World Wide Web Wanderer`. His goal was to measure the growth of the Web by letting his crawler run at regular intervals. In June of 1993, his software found 130 websites, six months later 623, and two years later it reached 23,500 websites [56]. Today, the best estimates of the Web's size are calculated by combining together the number of pages found by various crawlers and using statistical data on the intersection of those crawls and the amount of pages that is usually believed to escape them. This is what Worldwidewebsize does.[2] Using the information coming from the crawler of Google and that of Bing, it provides the size of the indexed Web. It used to also employ information from Yahoo! search and Ask Geeves to provide better estimates, but unfortunately those two search engines stopped releasing crawl information to the public. Typically, the numbers generated in this way are an underestimation of the actual size [24].

What makes such estimations reasonably precise is that the Web is considered to be quite connected, meaning that following links is a sensible approach for finding most of the available content. In 1999, Andrei Broder

---

[2]http://www.worldwidewebsize.com.

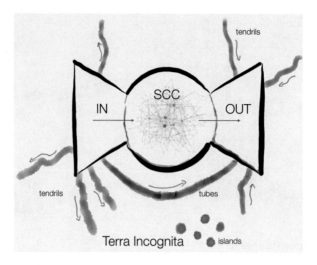

Fig. 9.2 The bow-tie model of the Web [27]

and colleagues, using a 200 million page crawl, gave an iconic representation of the "shape" of the Web, referring to it as a *bow-tie model* [27]. The model is based on the idea that there are essentially four types of pages. One type are those that are part of a strongly connected core (SCC in Fig. 9.2) known as the *Milgram continent*, with many links going from one to another and making the reaching of any page by following few links possible. They estimated 30% of the 200 million pages to fall into this category. Then there is a set of pages that attracts many links from a strongly connected core and is referred to as the *corporate continent* (OUT in Fig. 9.2). It is made up by about 20% of the pages and constitutes the right wing of the bow tie. Symmetrically, there is the *new archipelago* formed by the same amount of pages, and it has mostly outgoing links (marked as "IN" in Fig. 9.2). A great deal of these go to the strongly connected core, while a few form tubes that lead directly to the corporate continent. The remaining 20% of the pages are considered *terra incognita*, being tendrils leaving the new archipelago and either entering the corporate continent, or completely disconnecting from the bow tie and forming islands.

The crawl used in that study also allowed Broder and his colleagues to measure the distance between any two nodes. The distance is the number of links that has to be followed on average to go from one node to any other one. Excluding the disconnected components, this was measured as 6.83 edges, if edges are considered bidirectional, while if one can only follow links from source to target, the measure increases to slightly over 16 edges for 75% of the nodes, leaving no path for the remaining 25% [27].

9.2   Self-Organization and Complex Networks

Who designed the Web to be a bow-tie? Who decided that the average distance between any two Web pages should be roughly seven links? Actually, there is no one who designed the Web to have these properties and features, rather these have naturally emerged as the effect of the collective effort of all Web authors. Even though we all think of ourselves as unique, many of our actions are very likely to be similar. When we create a Web page about cars, most likely we put a link to the Ferrari website and to other prominent car manufacturers, as other people with similar inclinations as ours would do. When we set up a website about InPerFor, a bakelite toy from the 1950s, we are likely to attract links from collectors of historic toys, and so on. In other terms, our individual actions contribute to globally noticeable behaviors without us being aware of it nor following any specific instruction. This is not true just of the Web, but of many natural and human endeavors [94, 95].

Stanley Milgram was a famous American social psychologist that in the mid-1960s decided to experimentally test the structure of society as represented by the links between people who know each other. His experimental setup was as follows. He randomly picked 296 people in Nebraska and Kansas, asking them to relay a message to someone in Massachusetts. The instructions were to send the message to the target person directly, only if directly known. Otherwise, the message was to be sent to an acquaintance who was considered the most likely to know the target person. Each time that someone received a letter from the experiment, a postcard was sent to Milgram at Harvard in order for him to trace the progress of the experiment. Sixty four letters made it to the final destination; one took less than a week and used only two people to reach the target. On average, the letters that made it used 5.2 people. What Milgram found was experimental evidence that society, as witnessed by the acquaintance relationship among people, is a rather compact graph, where on average one needs about six hops to reach any other individual, a phenomenon that is also known as six degrees of separation [88, 109]. The SCC continent of the bow-tie model is named after him.

More recent studies have proposed graph models that are more elaborate, though are based on the same network idea. A popular one is the so called *Small-World model*, which came from the PhD research of Duncan Watts under the supervision of Steven Strogatz [118]. Small-World networks are characterized by having a limited number of nodes between any two nodes, but also a high clustering coefficient. The clustering coefficient captures the fact that friends of friends are likely to also be friends. Watts' original study was a model to explain the coordination mechanism of snowy tree crickets falling into a unison chirping state.

Again, who decided that human social structure or the way in which crickets coordinate, should follow such a model? Nobody. At most we can consider this an effect of evolution and natural selection. The story for the Web is similar. The Web has a characteristic structure that was not designed to be there, but its presence is extremely useful to understand the Web and to profit from it. The Web's structure is best modelled as a *scale-free network*. This means that its properties do not change significantly with the size of the graph. A Web of one million pages and one of a billion pages will both have a similar average distance between nodes, for instance. In most Web models, the *average path length (APL)* and the *characteristic path length (CPL)*[3] grow extremely slowly as the whole graph grows. Under certain conditions, the APL has been shown to grow proportionally to

$$\frac{log(n)}{log(log(n))}$$

that is, extremely slowly [38]. So if we start with a thousand nodes graph with APL of six, it is likely that the one billion nodes version of it will have an APL of just nine, and for the graph with 10^{18} nodes, it will be less than 14.

In 1999, Réka Albert and Albert-Laszló Barabasi proposed the *preferential attachment model* to describe the structure and growth of the Web [10]. The model comes from a stochastic process. One starts with a node, then adds a second one, and so on. Every time a new node is added, the links to existing nodes are created based on a probability that is a function of the number of edges the existing node already has. In other words, the nodes which already have many links are "preferred" and likely to get more, while the ones with few links will attract few newer links. The graph so created exhibits a number of interesting properties. The degree distribution follows a power law with an exponent of about 2.9, the average path length is the logarithm of the logarithm of the size, and a few nodes emerge as "hubs" collecting a great fraction of all the links. This is the most noticeable effect of the power law. Few nodes are rich in connectivity, and a vast majority of the node population has few links. In fact, the power law distribution is also known as the "rich get richer" or Pareto law.

---

[3]The characteristic path length is the median of the average of the minimum distance between any two nodes of the graph.

Vilfredo Pareto was an Italian scientist and economist who, among other things, had noticed that after reunification in the nineteenth century, 80% of Italian land was owned by 20% of the population. This 80/20 rule applies to many fields and is still true today for the wealth of most capitalistic countries. Sometimes, the few rich families change over generations. For instance, most of the current richest people are newcomers who have benefited from the emergence of ICT, while in other cases, over the generations the same few families own the same majority of wealth. This is the case of Florence where, in six centuries, the same families, as identified by their last name and professions, have kept a large part of the wealth. In a study starting with tax data from 1421, two economists of the Italian Central Bank have analyzed wealth and tax data to come to such a conclusion [13]. If incoming links on the Web can be considered wealth, then we can say that the Pareto observations fit the Web very well. Most likely, the traffic on the Web also follows a similar law, where a few hot websites are very frequently visited, while a huge number of pages seldom are, if at all, visited. The most visited ones currently are Google, YouTube, Facebook, Baidu, and Wikipedia.

The *copying model* refines the idea of preferential attachment by considering existing Web nodes as prototypes for new ones [69]. The growth process goes as follows: With probability β, a new node adds edges to existing nodes uniformly at random. With probability $1 - \beta$, the node copies the edges from an existing node chosen at random. The model is slightly more accurate than the preferential attachment model, as it captures the likelihood that a page is similar to another one. If one is creating a page about cars, one may be inspired by an existing one to improve on, or anyway, it is likely that one will end up putting links to many of the same pages as the existing page about cars. The copying model exhibits properties of scale-freeness, the node degree distribution follows a power law with an exponent of about 2.4, and it has a small CPL.

Figure 9.3 gives three examples of graphs generated following the Small-World, the preferential attachment, and the copying model, respectively. One notices the compact nature of the first model, with many identifiable triangles. The second graph has a few highly connected hubs (larger circles in the figure). Likewise, the third graph has a few hubs and structures that seem to repeat themselves throughout the graph.

Identifying the structure and models for the growth of the Web goes beyond an intellectual exercise. Information on the self-organization of the Web can be very useful for working with it, especially for finding information. In fact, the distributed nature of content generation for the Web and the absence of indices, make the retrieval of information cumbersome.

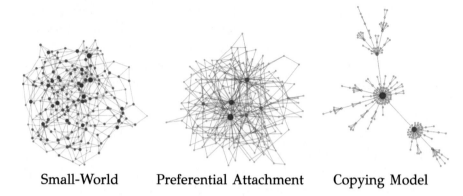

Small-World   Preferential Attachment   Copying Model

Fig. 9.3 Examples of graphs built following well-known models

9.3   Searching the Web

The Web of 1992 had less than ten websites. One could easily remember all of them by heart. In 1995, the range jumped to the tens of thousands. How could one find a desired page? The Web has no provision for the indexing of content beyond the URL scheme for addressing resources, that is, URLs only contain the HTML file name and the host address, and no extra information. There is no central index of terms or resolution scheme to translate terms or metadata into page addresses. The distributed nature of the Web makes the creation of such an index translation system cumbersome and makes it virtually impossible to keep it up to date. *Web Search Engines* emerged early in Web history as the tool to use in combination with the Web to find relevant information. To some extent they can also be considered a patch to the original Web pattern. Search engines address a user-related issue rather than a computational one. Therefore, I do not give them the status of a computational patch, as done for the other innovations presented in Chaps. 6–8.

In the early days of the Web, the most precious resource of a Web navigator was the collection of links saved as bookmarks. These were typically built over long periods of Web navigation and often posted on one's own Web page. Once a relevant and useful website was found, one had to bookmark it immediately, even if retrieved with a search engine. The very same engine could give an entirely different sets of results for the same query the very next day. The approach went beyond the individual keeping her own bookmarks organized, and was also the method of a major search engine of the time. Yahoo! was originally built on the concept of a manually edited directory with human-generated annotations to help navigate it. Admittedly time consuming, but providing results of a quality not reachable by the automatic systems of the time.

$\sim$

The field of *Information Retrieval* is dedicated to the task of finding information in large, complex data sets, may these be structured (e.g., relational databases) or unstructured (e.g., collections of textual documents). A pioneer in the area of textual information retrieval for large text collections was Gerard Salton. A professor of computer science at Harvard first, Cornell later, he initiated and led a pioneering project called *System for the Mechanical Analysis and Retrieval of Text (SMART)*. The main novelty of the approach proposed by Salton was that it considered a vector space made of all the terms occurring in the document collection, then every document could be represented as a vector, possibly weighted by document term frequency. User queries are also represented as vectors of the words inputted by the user, and the search functionality is interpreted as finding the document vectors which are the most similar to the query, that is, have the smallest angle to the query vector. These principles survive today in modern search engines.

The first "search engine" to hit the Web used much simpler techniques. In 1992, the `Archie` system developed by Alan Emtage at the McGill University was turned to Web archiving. Developed from 1987 as a system to store listings of FTP sites, it was extended to also keep an archive of Web URLs. It was based on regular expression keyword matching and ended up being a database of known URLs. The search for matches included the HTML of the stored Web pages. Updates to the database were automatically carried out by a script running at McGill. A year later, Martijn Koster created `Aliweb`, which included a crawler to automatically find Web pages and also the possibility for people to submit URLs of their pages together with a description of their content. In 1994, `Excite` saw its birth, from the intuitions of six Stanford undergraduate students. Excite was the first engine to gain popularity and to use term frequency and word correlation in documents to improve the quality of the results.

In the same period, two graduate students at Stanford were collecting URLs for their own entertainment and manually annotating information regarding their content. The directory was called `Yahoo!` and attracted an increasing number of people to browse it. The quality of the manual annotation provided an added value for the finding of authoritative websites on specific topics. Yahoo! then started charging commercial companies to appear in their directory and became an important player in the search engine market. Two more important players came to the scene around 1995. `Infoseek` was a popular search engine, especially after partnering with Netscape and becoming its default search engine. Altavista brought important innovations by allowing free natural language queries, and the checking of inbound links to pages crawled. As a result, it became the most popular search engine in 1997.

The field made a major leap ahead when, in 1998, a new player, called Google, coming from another two Stanford graduate students, saw the light. In late 1995, Larry Page was starting on his PhD research and was considering the problem of identifying links pointing to any given page. His PhD advisor and human-computer interaction expert, Terry Winograd, encouraged him to pursue the matter further. He then started a project called BackRub. Page considered links to be a kind of Web page citation which, as in bibliometrics, defines a measure of importance of the referenced paper [14]. He soon attracted a mathematically talented colleague to join the effort, Sergei Brin, and the two set to work on the problem [115].

The project proposed a concept of ranking pages based on the importance of the incoming links, that is, a page is important if it is referenced by other important pages. Even though the definition is circular, it can actually be used in practice. One can translate it into a discrete stochastic process representing the likelihood that a random Web surfer will end up on a given page [74]. Pages which are important have a higher likelihood of being visited and give importance to the pages they link to. It is not just a counting of which page has the most links, but it also includes a qualification of the links. Only links coming from important pages have large positive contribution to the importance of pages they link to. Page and Brin called *PageRank* the measure of the relevance of a page, that is, the probability that, among all Web pages, it will be visited by a Web surfer [26]. The idea of PageRank is not new [50]. In bibliometrics, a 1976 definition proposes the impact of a journal as the number of citations it receives from important journals [99]. In sociometry, a 1949 proposal sets the important people to be the ones endorsed by important people [102]. Leontief's 1941 input/output model of material and production sectors is based on a similar definition of importance and earned him a Nobel prize for economics [79].

PageRank was a major improvement to search engine technology because it allowed retrieval systems to go beyond the mere page content, but to also consider its position in the Web graph network. It is more refined than the counting of the incoming links to the pages, the in-degree; it represents a distribution of importance among all nodes based on the overall topology. PageRank is an emerging property of the Web graph. Like the bow-tie-shape of the Web, the presence of hubs, and the scale-free nature, no individual decides what the PageRank of a page should be, but it rather emerges from the collective effort of providing Web content and links, in particular. One may wonder how PageRank is distributed among Web pages. Interestingly, it has been shown to follow a power law, much like the average node degree [17]. That is, few very important pages exist and a vast amount of pages with PageRank close to zero complete the Web.

PageRank is a value that can be easily translated into money. If the owner of a website transforms every ten visits into one physical product sale, it is clear that increasing the number of visits will increase sales. Since PageRank models the likelihood of being visited, then the owners should try to improve the PageRank of their own websites. Given the wide interest in doing this, many "tricks" have been exploited to increase it. People add links to the pages they want to push anywhere they can, for instance in open discussion forums or by creating extra websites. Some of the tricks do not last long, as search engines and W3C come with appropriate countermeasures. For instance, the `nofollow` attribute has been added to links appearing in blogs to let search engines know that the links should not count toward the computation of PageRank. In 2004, a group of individuals created a set of pages with high PageRank and with text associated with the Web page of American president G. W. Bush. The detonation of what is known as a *Google bomb* was successful, and the search engine would bring up the president's website as the first hit when the keywords "miserable failure" were inputted. A similar stunt had been pulled as early as 1999 to bring searchers for "more evil than Satan himself" to the homepage of Microsoft.

Marco Gori and colleagues have created a model of PageRank that represents it as energy. The more energy a node can attract and retain, the more PageRank it has. According to this model, it is best to have few outgoing links, to avoid pages without outgoing links (they act as dissipators and burn energy, or more precisely, they force the Web surfer to perform a random jump to another page), and to divide content over more interlinked pages [21].

PageRank is a topological measure of the quality of a node; therefore it is a static graph property. Given a Web graph, the value of PageRank per node is uniquely determined, independently of what people will actually do on the Web. Measures based on actual traffic have been shown to be more effective in determining page relevance and to be computationally slightly more expensive than PageRank, though still practically usable [74]. A traffic-based ranking system models popularity as heat of nodes. The more traffic a node receives, the hotter it gets. If computing a traffic-based ranking is feasible, the largest problem resides in the acquisition of traffic data. Owning a popular browser platform and requesting all users to share their traffic data would provide an excellent sample of traffic to compute such ranking, though legitimate privacy concerns hinder the appeal of such approaches on a global scale.

9.4   Self-Organization, Patching, and the Role of Amateurs

Unlike natural spiderwebs, where one spider weaves its own individual web for residence and nourishment purposes, one electronic Web is shared by a multitude of independent human and software spiders. These act autonomously according to their own individual goals, though still collectively leave patterns and global properties that clearly emerge when looking to the Web. Even the five patches that we have identified so far, described in Chaps. 6–8 as major evolutions to the original Web pattern, come from different and independent sources.

Cookies originated from the need of a Netscape client; Java came from the efforts of Sun Microsystems on object-oriented languages; Flash technology came from the computer graphics company Adobe; Microsoft proposed the Silverlight framework for dynamic Web content and active XMLHttpRequest; and Web Services originated from IBM, SAP, and other prominent traditional ICT companies. Beyond existing ICT companies, entirely new companies started up with business goals tied to the Web and proposed patches for their own business needs. Search engines have filled the gap left by the lack of centralized Web indexing by providing ever more refined search tools.

One may be left to wonder if the flourishing of distributed efforts to work and evolve the Web came from the original Web pattern lacking many features. Was the amateuristic original design what attracted so much attention from many small and big players? Or was it rather its rapid success? It is hard to provide a final answer to this question, as there is evidence to sustain both of these hypotheses. This book argues that certain design decisions could have been better, especially when considering the state of the art in computer science. It views patching as a necessary and urgent cure. One can counter-argue with equal validity that the Web was successful because it was simple, open, and encouraged wide participation from the community first, and from anybody interested later. Perhaps it was not an amateuristic design, but rather a necessary and winning simplicity.

The *end-to-end argument* proposed by Jerry Saltzer, David Reed, and David Clark in 1984 may also be relevant here [101]. Based on a series of experiences with networked applications at MIT, the authors suggest that even well-engineered layered architectures may cause high inefficiency in development and operation of systems. Working at the application level is the most practical and effective solution. To bring the argument to the Web case, the reasoning goes that a very well-designed system would have been impractical or impossible to build—like Xanadu—while something like the Web with a simple application level pattern and related technologies was the right way to success. Former director of technology at Netscape Communications, Martin Haeberli, points out that this is in fact the case also for the Internet. While prominent scientists and technologists were working on a beautiful, layered model of internetworking, the ISO/OSI seven layer model [125], the Internet came about, which worked just fine and had basically half of the layers of the official model. In Martin's own words, the ISO/OSI Networking model was a Tower of Babel, "intended to be a beautiful and powerful architecture, but it collapsed under its own weight and was never realized."[4] The Semantic Web's destiny may turn out in a similar way. In contrast with the simplicity and extendability of the original Web pattern, the Semantic Web lacked ease of use, intuitive functionalities, and easy-to-exploit business models. Finally, it was never widely adopted.

There is yet another possible interpretation to the success of the Web that is independent of the amateur vs. the professional design. What if the Web was simply the statistically blessed grain of sand to start the landslide and impact the sandpile? In the early 1990s, the world was ready for a great application to run over the Internet, and hypertextuality was receiving increasing attention in the academic and entrepreneurial communities. In that period, many proposals were appearing and consolidating: Xanadu, Trigg's Textnet, Brown University's Intermedia, Gopher, HyperCard, and…the Web [41].

In his book, the physicist Per Bak proposes a model of complex phenomena explained by simple rules of self-organization. The book, which goes by the unassuming title of How Nature Works, uses as its prominent example a sandpile to which one adds grains of sand at the top [9]. Grain after grain, the sandpile uniformly increases in size till the moment that one grain initiates a landslide, in turn, greatly reducing the pile's size. What is special of that grain that caused the major change? How can the phenomenon be described? According to Bak and colleagues, one can only come up with a statistical description which determines the likelihood of when the landslide will emerge, and there is nothing special about that grain of sand; it simply was its turn to go on the pile in a moment of criticality, with high chances of changing the

---

[4]Personal communication.

system it was part of. By following this argument, the Web was the grain of sand that initiated a major shift and change in the Internet world. Bak says that critical events are spot occurrences on extended timelines, which cause major changes to the system they occur in.

Looking through the glasses of the philosophy of science, one can see a parallel with the interpretation of science as a sequence of *paradigm shifts*. A model of science based on these was proposed by Thomas Kuhn in his book about THE STRUCTURE OF SCIENTIFIC REVOLUTIONS [72]. Kuhn's argument about science describes a similar phenomenon to the self-organized criticality where a field goes on with business as usual for long periods of time until the moment that the world is ready for a paradigm shift in the same way that type of science is done. When a shift occurs, it is both rapid and radical.

It is difficult, if worthwhile at all, to understand the Web through the lens of the argument of an amateuristic design vs. simplicity and being present at the right place at the right time. It is rather better to keep an eye on the future and be visionaries concerning the direction that this magnificent, human, self-organized infrastructure can and will take, keeping in mind its history.

10

The Pervasive Future
At the Edge of a Web of Things

Tout devient digital et on ne peut plus rien toucher.
Zap Mama

Predicting the future is a perilous enterprise. The work of a lifetime can be forgotten in the face of a visionary yet unrealized prediction, and one's name remains forever associated with a popular quote that time proved wrong. In a fast-moving field such as that of computer science it is not only easy to make wrong predictions, but it is also possible to see them falsified in a few years' time.

The first IBM CEO, Thomas J. Watson, is quoted as having said in the middle of the previous century, "I see a market for at most five computers in the world," while the Microsoft founder Bill Gates is quoted as having said in 1981 that "640K [of RAM] ought to be enough for anybody." Interestingly, there is no documented evidence of Watson's quote, and Gates has explicitly denied having said the sentence attributed to him.

Tim Berners-Lee's prediction about the Semantic Web's potential and future adoption have also gone mostly unrealized. In his 1999 book, he writes, "Cynics have already said to me, 'You really think this time around people are going to pick up on the architecture, and spend hours and hours on it as Pei Wei and all the others did?' Yes. Because that's just what the cynics said in 1989. They said, 'Oh, well, this is just too much to take on.' But remember, it takes only a half dozen good people in the right places. Back then, finding that half dozen took a long time. Today, the world can come to the consortium, plug in their ideas, and have them disseminated" [19].

© Springer International Publishing AG, part of Springer Nature 2018
M. Aiello, *The Web Was Done by Amateurs*,
https://doi.org/10.1007/978-3-319-90008-7_10

Apparently, there are only two ways to avoid the risks of failing at predicting the future. The Alan Kay way has a clear recipe: "The best way to predict the future is to invent it." Most likely the most famous quote of Kay, and clearly one that he can afford to state due to his pioneering work on personal computing and object-oriented programming. The second way is that of abstinence. I will follow the latter. While I identify some trends in the current Web that can concretize in one of the possible futures of the Web, I will avoid making predictions as much as possible.

10.1 Apps

Consider again the growth of the Web presented in the previous chapter. In Fig. 9.1, the data is plotted on a linear scale and shows the impressive increase in website numbers. If we plot the same data on a logarithmic scale, as done in Fig. 10.1, one can notice something else. Clearly the exponential growth has characterized the whole history of the Web. In the first decade it was very vigorous, but it is now slowing down. By no means should this be interpreted as a sign of decline or the imminent end of the technology. What it does show is, at most, some signs of saturation. Is there a rival platform entering the scene? To some extent, the role of the Web for businesses at the end of the 1990s and early 2000s has now been taken over by mobile phone and tablet applications, by *apps*.

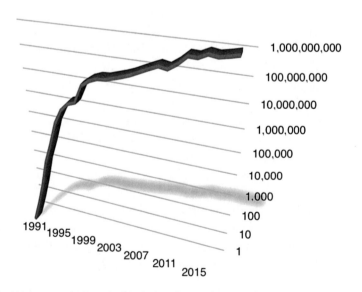

Fig. 10.1 Web growth since its birth on a logarithmic scale

Mobile phones have become compact and powerful computational devices. They have constant access to the Internet and are very frequently in the hands of their owners, including while deambulating. In most countries, Internet access via mobile phones has surpassed Internet access with desktop and laptop computers. The trend is noticeable beginning in 2008 and culminates with the overtaking by mobile devices. In the US, the takeover occurred in 2014. Not only is the mobile device increasingly employed, often it is the only Internet access used by individuals. The percentage can vary; it is around 10% for countries like the US, Canada, and the UK, while it reaches 25% for Italy and an astonishing 70% for Indonesia [36]. The trend has affected the Web. For about a decade, many websites have offered two versions: a version for desktops and laptops designed for full screen and mouse and keyboard interactions, and a more compact version for a smaller screen and possibly designed for finger and stylus interactions. The step from the mobile version to a dedicated phone application is relatively small.

Parallel to the increase in mobile versions of websites, mobile apps have conquered important mobile phone space. The Apple App Store provides an interesting example. In July 2008, about 300 apps were available, but by the end of 2016, the number rose to over two millions. The full progress is shown in Fig. 10.2, where the data refers to Apple's June yearly announcements. Broadening the view, the total number of downloaded apps on all major app platforms (Google Play, Apple Store, Windows Microsoft) in 2016 has neared the 150 billion mark. If for a competitive company 10–15 years ago it was

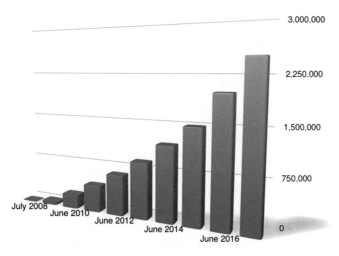

Fig. 10.2 Number of apps available on the Apple "App Store"

mandatory to have a website, today it is equally essential to have a mobile app presence. To a large extent, an app has the same function a Web page had before: it offers services from the company and information about it.

Moving from the website to the app may be a straightforward enterprise. In fact, HTML 5, the latest version of Tim Berners-Lee's original specification, is a flexible Web description language that works magnificently for websites and can also easily be deployed within apps. This means that interacting with a Web page from a PC, from a mobile device's Web browser, and from an app are very similar experiences. Porting a website to an app directly using HTML 5 also helps to address multiple platforms at once (Android, iOS, Windows Mobile, etc.). On the other hand, a solution based on HTML 5 and HTTP connections at the level of the app misses opportunities.

An app on a mobile phone can access important hardware and operating system resources. It is fully capable of performing client side computations and user interaction; it can store data on the client and have a full duplex socket-based connection. In other words, all the patches we have identified for the original Web are not necessary for the app world. For apps, there is some level of sandboxing preventing applications from performing certain operations on the phone. These typically require an explicit user authorization. Nevertheless the computational potential of an app is much higher than that of a Web page constrained inside a Web browser.

While there appears to be a convergence between apps and websites—especially mobile versions of them—it is fair to say that apps are eroding Web usage. Often people refer only to the app and ignore the Web version of a business service. According to Flurry analytics, a Yahoo! subsidiary, the amount of time spent on apps vs. the Web on mobile devices is about 80–20 and increasing. This means that if you are reading a Facebook post on your mobile device, it is more likely that you are using the Facebook app rather than the Web mobile version. By now, Amazon has more sales through the app than the website [67]. A number of people interpret this trend as the inevitable sign of the Web's imminent death [89].

It is clear that apps provide an important advantage to the companies creating them. The control over the data produced and managed by the app is higher, while it is possible to provide more services to the user. There is also another hidden advantage, the possibility to lock-in customers more easily. Jumping from Web page to Web page across domains of multiple companies is much easier and faster, than trying to switch between the mobile apps of competing companies once already inside one. In technical terms, following a link in the browser is orders of magnitude faster than an app context switch.

If from the computational point of view apps appear to be a better solution than websites, there are a number of critical points about them. First, apps are not an operating system for the mobility of objects as envisioned by Kay. The inter-app compatibility is non-existent. There are no standard semantics or data exchange formats. Apps tend not to talk to each other, and when they do, they resort to external data formats, e.g., PDF documents and email MIME formats. Second, the apps often serve a lock-in purpose. We can view apps as a very limited Web browser, one that allows the user to only interact with the website of the app developer. It's like going to the website of a car manufacturing company and not being allowed to search for competing manufacturers unless leaving the website. The app is a browser with limited freedom. The app creator unilaterally decided what to present to the user and what to allow. Third, the openness and self-organization of the Web is largely compromised in the app world. The app platforms and distribution are dominated by two giants: Google and Apple with their respective stores. They make margins on the apps, they decide what can and should appear on the stores, and they decide which apps to support and promote. The two tech firms, followed by Microsoft, are clearly monopolizing the sector.

Decreeing the death of the Web as the effect of the emergence of apps and the booming penetration of mobile devices appears to be too strong a conclusion. The two platforms are strongly connected and definitely influence each other. Apps have conquered some of the Web space, though they serve slightly different purposes. Some suggest that apps are for loyal users while mobile websites are for outreach [67]. One could also conclude that the apps are yet another patch to the Web, or better, a major redesign that encompasses all first four patches that we have identified in this book.

10.2 Web (on the Internet) of Things

Apps are a strong influence on the evolution of the current Web. In the previous section, we saw how they are actually substituting the Web browser to offer specific website and service navigation. HTML 5 technology can also be used to do just that—fit mobile content inside an app. Even if one codes an app rather than mere HTML rendering within an app, there is still an important role for Web technology. HTTP connections within apps and data exchange with proprietary clouds and databases is a typical design pattern for apps.

There is another emerging set of apps, those that connect to "things." Many of these take advantage of mobile devices' near field connections and direct object interfaces. Protocols and technologies such as Bluetooth, ZigBee, and NFC support the creation of small ad hoc-networks between mobile devices and things that have an electronic component. Watches and other wearable devices provide fitness information to apps, home appliances such as smart thermostats and LED-based lighting systems talk directly to phones, and dishwashers directly notify phones of the end of a washing cycle.

In other terms, there is a clear increase in everyday objects having a digital presence. Their state is captured electronically and can be invoked and changed via message passing. This creates a Web of devices that are physically close to each other and that can potentially cooperate. Such digitally rich spaces are often called *smart spaces*, while the infrastructure based on networked devices is presently referred to as the *Internet of Things*, on which the Web of Things builds. The term smart space has gained popularity and is considered a synonym to previous ones such as *Pervasive Computing* and the original *Ubiquitous Computing*. Interestingly, the latter also comes from Xerox PARC labs, more than a decade after the work on the DynaBook and SmallTalk of Alan Kay.

In 1987, Mark Weiser joined Xerox PARC. As introduced in Chap. 4, he coined the term Ubiquitous Computing to refer to a number of innovative technologies "that disappear" [119]. He considered the desktop computer emergence of the 1980s as something transitory and proposed a future where people are helped by technology that is calmly hidden in the environment. Similar to Engelbart's inspiration, people need support; Weiser's take is that the computer is quiet, invisible, and extending people's conscious and unconscious capabilities. Technologies should create calmness, like a walk in the forest, like nature. Weiser's vision was of an office space populated by hundred of devices with screens of all sizes, from one inch to full walls, where badges help identify people and gain authorization to access resources. To achieve his vision, he pointed to several crucial subareas of computer science: operating systems, user interfaces, networking, wireless communication, displays, and visualization. Perhaps understanding the difficulties of his time in achieving the full vision of Artificial Intelligence, he reassures that "no revolution in artificial intelligence is needed, merely computers embedded in the everyday world." Kay refers to ubiquitous computing as proposed by Weiser as the "Third Paradigm" to computing.

The vision of Weiser is very much current and, after 30 years, to a good extent, realized. It has affected more than the working office space, which was the focus of most of the original work of Weiser and his group, penetrating our daily lives beyond work. Today, we talk of smart homes, smart buildings, smart energy grids, smart devices, smart appliances, smart everything—really. I bet that if Web services were introduced today, they would be called *smart services*.

Ubiquitous computing has gone beyond the work space and the gadgets for the wealthy early adopters. Today, applications in the area of healthcare and physical performance enhancement are common. Many people wear inexpensive, health monitoring devices that collect data useful to monitor health conditions, support healthy lifestyles, and enhance athletic performances. Similarly, home smart appliances increase the safety of people at home by connecting security cameras and alarm detectors to the network, and improve comfort by adapting temperature and light conditions to the presence of people in the homes, overall increasing the comfort, safety, and sustainability of home living.

The Web was born as an infrastructure for information exchange between humans, to support the information retrieval and navigation. The introduction of things to the Web does not provide additional features for the fruition of information, rather it provides additional information and that essential contact point between the virtual and the physical worlds. Hyperlinks are useful at the conceptual level and much less in the physical world. On the other hand, it is extremely interesting to have links that point to physical sensors and actuators, to actual things. From a more technological point of view, the Web (or, more properly, the Internet) of Things easily integrates into the three-tier architecture presented in Chap. 5 in Fig. 4.2, as shown in Fig. 10.3. In fact, things can directly provide information to a server or a cloud via network links, or go through the client to upload information to the server, in the spirit of an

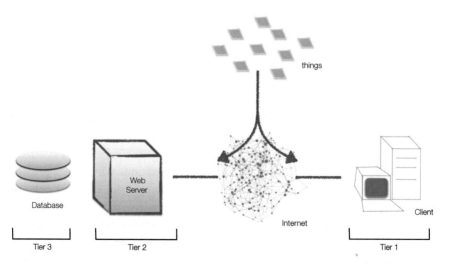

Fig. 10.3 The integration of Web (on the Internet) of Things into the three-tier architecture

Edge Computing approach (Fig. 7.5). In a few cases, the things communicate exclusively with the client without any interaction with a server or cloud.

10.3 The Web and Artificial Intelligence

In Chap. 3, we saw how the main motivation behind creating innovative information systems was to improve and support human cognitive capabilities. Engelbart was concerned with a world increasing in complexity that required people to be helped, Nelson was frustrated with the idea of sequential text on paper and marked it as unnatural, and Berners-Lee found it unnecessarily difficult to deal with a complex organization such as CERN. Even when considering the ubiquitous computing vision of Weiser, the motivation is to support employees and workers with cognitive tools. In other terms, none of these visionaries seemed concerned with providing systems with autonomous cognitive capabilities, with mechanized reasoning abilities, with *Artificial Intelligence*. At the same time, the systems and tools that have been introduced, such as the Web and its patches, can be fundamental to the creation of Artificial Intelligence.

Consider again the IBM Watson system cited in Sect. 8.3. The system is built to be able to verbally interact with humans as an expert. To demonstrate its ability, it played the American television game Jeopardy! competing with two human champions. In order to score in the game, the players need to provide the right question to clues presented to them as answers. In 2011, IBM Watson played against the two human champions Ken Jennings and Brad Rutter in a two-game match, which were both won by the computer system. IBM Watson used state of the art Artificial Intelligence and natural language processing techniques, while it based most of its knowledge base on information gathered from the Web. The data was collected off-line, as during the actual competition IBM Watson was not allowed to connect to any external network, including the Internet.

The Web is a fabulous field for Artificial Intelligence systems. It is a place where it is easy to gather huge amounts of information, where it is possible to interact with services thanks to reasonably standardized interfaces. We saw in Sect. 7.5 how with an AI Planning system one can create adaptive service compositions. It is a place where the abundance and redundancy of data and information help train machine learning systems. It is a place where one can interact digitally with humans, thus reducing the difficulties tied to embodiment and physical interaction typical of AI robotics systems.

Artificial Intelligence shares a great part of its history with that of computing science. There are two milestones tied to its birth. The first is Alan Turing's 1950 paper on machine intelligence where, among other things, he provides a definition of a thinking machine. It is one that, when interacting with a human, will be mistaken for another human rather than recognized as a machine. This is famously known as the *Turing test*, and up to now, it is still widely considered a fundamental test of intelligence for machines [110]. The second milestone is the 1956 workshop, titled AI, held at Dartmouth College. There a number of eminent scientists showcased their initial results in systems playing checkers, generating text, and proving mathematical theorems. The field was born, and soon AI Labs around the world would see the light of day.

Initial approaches to AI had a lot in common with formal logic. The core idea was the mechanization of reasoning as formal proof systems, that is, a symbolic approach to intelligence. One can represent facts as formulas and perform reasoning with mechanisms as deduction, resolution, abduction, etc. Once a system is built with such foundations, it is typically easy to prove properties and know the system's pros and cons by design.

The field of Artificial Intelligence has been seasonal since its birth. It started as a sunny and summery beginning for a period going from the 1950s to the 1980s. In that season, large funding was available and promises of systems being able to compete with humans and win on almost any level dominated. Critical voices recurred, pointing at the unfeasibility of the promises, but were mostly isolated. In the 1980s, the focus shifted from general purpose systems, to specialized solutions for specific areas, e.g., for medical diagnosis. Though systems were built and proven effective, they were quite expensive and often required specialized, costly hardware. This was the autumn, with initial signs of a winter approaching. From the mid-1980s, the critique that AI promises seemed too ambitious and unrealistic was gaining momentum, and the field fell into what is known as its deep winter. A season of little funding and contraction of the discipline. Signs of spring could only be appreciated from the 1990s. A number of challenges promised 50 years back were won. John McCarthy's prediction that the world chess champion would be beaten by a computer within five decades came true in 1997, with IBM Deep Blue defeating the human world champion, Gary Kasparov. In 2005, five cars completed the autonomous driving desert track of the DARPA Grand Challenge. In 2016, AlphaGo defeated the world champion of the Japanese board game Go. This gradually brought AI to a new summer, though a very different summer.

Artificial Intelligence was seen as a futuristic world full of potential in its initial phases. However, during the cyclic winters, it has acquired a negative connotation, a word used to define a useless research project and waste of resources. Currently, it is again a positive word, even used to promote ideas beyond academic research to industrial and societal parties. The current approach is very far from the original symbolic one. The statistical road to AI is dominating. The rationale behind it is that there are large amounts of data, often unstructured, available that serve the purpose of learning automatically, and therefore creating systems that behave intelligently by imitation.

The Web is for sure one of the most opulent sources of semi-structured data, though not the only one. Physical sensors are becoming equally generous in providing data. For instance, the number of video-cameras installed around the world is believed to be above 250 million, millions of smart meters measure electricity flows, tens of millions of road sensors measure traffic, mobile phone cells know about the movement and behavior of billions of phone owners, and so on. Data, especially when abundant, is then exploited for automatic learning purposes. Given a set of data and some evidence extracted from it either by hand or semiautomatically, one can train a system to work on any new data. For example, showing a system how one drives a car for hours and hours will provide clues on how to automate driving, and ultimately deliver an autonomous driving system.

Such machine learning approaches on large amounts of data, or big data, is proving increasingly successful in solving real problems. Artificial Intelligence is no longer seen as a denigratory term, but as a marketing one. Hopes for autonomous intelligent systems are again on the rise. Expectations are so strong, that some people are currently worried that AI systems will take over humanity, that the next dominating species on earth is a robotic one, while humans are doomed to extinction. A slightly more positive variant is that robots are the natural evolution of the human species and that the biological and technological species will happily coexist.

These enthusiastic visions and concerns are legitimate, but must be pondered carefully. AI progress of the last decades is definitely tied to the growth and popularity of the Web; techniques concerning information retrieval have become more and more popular and have had a deep influence on Artificial Intelligence. We certainly have better systems today, and we can deploy them to take care of an increasing number of tasks. At the same time, we are losing some control over the systems. Too often we create a system that learns, that performs a task very well, but for which we can hardly provide a description of its "reasoning" strategy. In other terms, we can explain how it learned, but not what it learned.

It is interesting to also consider the artistic view on AI, as presented in successful and well-thought, science fiction movies. In *2001: A Space Odyssey,*

Blade Runner, or the more recent *Ex Machina,* AI artifacts are basically indistinguishable from the naturally intelligent humans and are often also embedded into human-like bodies. But such intelligence inevitably, and inexplicably, leads to human murder. Stanley Kubrick, director and writer of *2001: A Space Odyssey,* was convinced that intelligence was indiscernible from violence, that they were almost synonyms. With the AI system, Hal, killing the astronauts towards the end of the movie, he actually provides evidence for his belief of a violent intelligence. It is as if a new sort of Turing test is defined, a macabre one. Is murder the ultimate test to prove artificial intelligence? A popular sci-fi writer, Isaac Asimov, is credited for introducing the word *robot*, and also for defining the laws that robots must obey. The rules, introduced in his 1942 short story RUNAROUND are repeated in the 1950 book I, ROBOT: MAN-LIKE MACHINES RULE THE WORLD! are the following three: [7]

1. A robot may not injure a human being or, through inaction, allow a human being to come to harm.
2. A robot must obey the orders given it by human beings except where such orders would conflict with the First Law.
3. A robot must protect its own existence as long as such protection does not conflict with the First or Second Laws.

The scientist, the inventor, and the engineer have the ambition to improve the world's welfare. This is true of all the people we have encountered in the present book. They want to be recognized for the impact made for a better world. The evil, insane scientist like Dr. Strangelove-Merkwerdichliebe is not common in real life. There are plenty of odd scientists out there, especially in computer science, but I have never met or heard of anyone who had murder or genocide as their goal. Personally, I love technology, science, and thinking of future needs and solutions where technology supports the human. In 2016, Alexander Lazovik, Faris Nizamic, Tuan Anh Nguyen, and myself founded the company, SustainableBuildings. The idea of the company is to save energy in commercial and public buildings by automating energy management, by bringing smartness, if not intelligence, to building usage. The core smartness comes from techniques similar to those used for service composition (see Sect. 7.5). I like technology that can turn things on and off, trying to understand what the human needs. Every time a person overrules our system by turning on a light, opening a window, or just being dissatisfied with some automatism, we have lost. Every joule of energy we save without bothering the user or, even better, by improving the user's experience, comfort, and productivity, we have won.

This system can hardly harm anybody; at most it may annoy people by not providing the right comfort level. Though in other contexts, the laws of Asimov become relevant and ethically challenging. Self-driving cars are a nice example of ethical dilemmas. What if a car is in a situation in which, no matter what action it takes, it will injure or kill people? Say it is driving at 100 km/h, when a group of pedestrians walks into the middle of the road, which is otherwise surrounded by high cement walls. Braking is not an option, as the people are too close. So either hit the pedestrians, most likely killing them all, or hit the wall, most likely killing the car occupants. Does this break the first law of Asimov? More generally, can we build AI systems that learn from Web data and provably will not violate any of Asimov's laws?

11

Should a New Web Be Designed?
The Greenfield Utopia

The temptation of any engineer when facing the challenge of building something out of an existing system is to demolish everything and to start from scratch. It is only natural to want total liberty of design and want the hands free from any constraint coming from legacy material. Doing so is usually unrealistic, unfeasible, and most of all, wasteful. In as much as one can agree with Kay in criticizing the ability of distributed computation and object mobility of the first and even the current Web, it takes more than a visionary to consider an entirely new Web to the current one. It requires traits most often found in megalomaniacs. The type of person who would go to the speaker's corner in Hyde Park in a desperate search for attention.

The Web is an evolving system, as we have seen in Chap. 9. A beautiful, self-organized one that owes its existence to the contribution of a great number of independent and free people. The real goal is thus not that of designing a new Web, but rather predicting what features one needs to improve performance, efficiency, and in turn global welfare and societal fairness. In other words, facilitating the Web towards becoming a natural resource, too, like the Pacific Ocean Internet.

In the present book, we have focused on computational patches, and we saw how much the Web has changed with respect to the computational load between client and server. We have deemed security issues to be out of scope, as they are. Though it is important to notice that security is also an area where major evolution has occurred and much more is needed. The ARPANET first, the Internet after, and the Web following have all been designed with trustworthy parties in mind. After all, the excitement of having computers

© Springer International Publishing AG, part of Springer Nature 2018
M. Aiello, *The Web Was Done by Amateurs*,
https://doi.org/10.1007/978-3-319-90008-7_11

cooperate with each other over a network was so strong that nobody thought of malicious and irresponsible components being connected, too.

As soon as the system became open, the curiosity and malevolence of some individuals showed how weak the system design was in terms of security. Even well-designed systems like HyperCard suffered from security attacks. In 1991, the first Hypercard virus was discovered in the Benelux. The usual security and trust issues continue to occur. Can someone eavesdrop on a communication? Can someone intervene in a communication and change the content of the messages? Can someone impersonate someone else and try to gain access to precious or confidential resources?

The original Web design has no provisions to answer these questions negatively, and we have seen many exploits. A recent example is the use of JavaScript code embedded into Web pages that takes advantage of the client computer to mine cryptocurrencies. While a user is visiting a Web page, the HTML contains extra JavaScript code that performs computations which are useful to whomever provided the page, but are irrelevant to the user.

When information about such mischievous use of the Web hits the news, it is often the case that technology is scrutinized and advocates of controlling, or even shutting down, the Web appear. Nothing surprising, it is the usual controversy between a useful technology and its malevolent use. Is nuclear power good or bad? Well, it can provide high amounts of relatively clean energy, but it can also be used to create deadly, very powerful bombs. Are pillows good or bad? Well, they are soft and cozy; but they can be used to suffocate someone in their sleep. Is the Web good or bad? Well …

There are additional issues of trustworthiness of the sources. Anybody can put up a website and share information, true or false as it may be. Anybody can forge an existing website and try to impersonate someone else's services, phishing being a classic example. There is no real authority and credential checking on the Web. To some extent, PageRank addresses this issue statistically by providing a likelihood of trustworthiness of a source, but again, we have seen how a Google bomb can exploit even that as a trust mechanism. Recent political elections have been affected by false news spreading during the campaign. If rumor spreading is part of human nature, the Web and other platforms are threatening due to the rapidity and scale at which they can help a possibly false rumor to spread.

There are no obvious solutions to patch all security and trust threats on the Web. Netscape came early with the introduction of encryption for client-server interactions (Secure Sockets Layer, SSL, in 1994). The domain name translation system appears to be a weak link in the Web infrastructure. "It has become apparent that, in addition to a need to expand the Internet address space through the introduction of IP version 6, with its 340 trillion trillion trillion addresses, there is also a strong need to introduce various security-enhancing mechanisms such as the *Domain Name System Security Extension (DNSSEC)* among many others" [47]. And many more patches and proposals have emerged and will have to emerge in the future.

We have seen how the computational landscape has also evolved dramatically since the original introduction of the Web. The evolution has seen an increase of computational capabilities being associated with the hypertextual nature of the original pattern. The client and the browser have hosted the core of the changes, becoming capable of storing data, running scripts, and proactively requesting content on open channels. It is safe to say that the Web has gone and is going towards that computational infrastructure dreamed by many. Not yet up to the standards of Kay, but at least in that direction. The Web is far from being a network of object containers where objects are riding around on top of networking packets and free to compose with each other on a per need basis. Perhaps this is an utopic view altogether, requiring levels of security that we cannot yet guarantee.

The world seems to take the statistical route these days at the expense of the formal symbolic one. Will this trend continue indefinitely and finally kill the ambition of a Web of moving programmable objects? It is hard to say. A major setback could occur at some point in the form of a catastrophic failure, though more likely, it will be possible to build an object/application layer on top of the machine learning-data rich layer that is currently dominating.

The Web, in its tireless evolution, is a vibrant field to study, an indispensable tool, and a wonderful playing field. This exciting infrastructure comes from the ideas, efforts, and visions of a vast number of people. Professionals and amateurs join forces and bring their contributions. The individual additions are indistinguishable from the outside, and most likely, from the inside, too. What we learned from revisiting the history of the Web is that nothing appears and succeeds purely by chance. Things evolve. Many proposals appear, build on each other, and compete to gain popularity. Kay's quotes help us once more: "If you don't fail at least 90% of the time, you're not aiming high enough." And indeed, the hypermedia is a field where we saw many attempts, few failures, and one major success, the Web. History proves that amateurism is not a killing factor; it appears that more decisive factors are perseverance, enthusiasm, and openness. The introduction of the Web has been a major technological and societal revolution. Another one will sooner or later occur, and no one can tell with certainty what will be the grain of sand to initiate it, to start the landslide, maybe an expert one or an amateuristic one—in our case, it did not matter.

~

The Web has become an integral and indispensable part of our daily lives. It has evolved with our society in the last 30 years at an incredible pace. It is hard to know what the Web of the future will look like, but it will be there in one form or another. Maybe the future Web will be the fuel of the background knowledge of a multitude of artificially intelligent agents that will talk to us, that will reason with us, that will support us. Maybe it will be a pervasive infrastructure that collects data from our offices, our homes, and our cars, so as to make our lives more safe, comfortable, and hassle-free. Maybe it will be a dynamic data repository that our brains can directly and effortlessly access via our sensory system or a direct brain-computer physical interface.

Correction to: The Web Was Done by Amateurs

Marco Aiello

Correction to:
M. Aiello, *The Web Was Done by Amateurs*,
https://doi.org/10.1007/978-3-319-90008-7

Some chapters in the initially published version contain a wrong affiliation of the author.

The correct affiliation of the author Marco Aiello is: University of Stuttgart, Stuttgart, Germany.

The affiliation has been corrected.

The updated online version of this book can be found at
https://doi.org/10.1007/978-3-319-90008-7

© Springer International Publishing AG, part of Springer Nature 2018
M. Aiello, *The Web Was Done by Amateurs*,
https://doi.org/10.1007/978-3-319-90008-7_12

A

Dr. Dobb's Interview with Alan Kay

Dr. Dobb's Website, July 10, 2012

A.1   A Note About Dr. Dobb's Journal

The Dr. Dobb's journal was a very popular magazine among programmers. Launched in 1976, it was the first software-oriented monthly magazine targeting practitioners. Unfortunately, December 2014 saw its last paper edition, while the website and code repository survive on-line. Most likely the magazine's existence was jeopardized by the Web itself, and the way advertising campaigns changed over the years.

I held a subscription for about a decade, starting in the mid-1990s. I even published a paper in it about Web-Service Notification with two undergraduate students in 2005 [5]. I jokingly refer to that paper as my most important scientific contribution. Could be. For sure, it is the only journal or magazine paper I ever wrote for which the publisher paid me.

© Springer International Publishing AG, part of Springer Nature 2018
M. Aiello, *The Web Was Done by Amateurs*,
https://doi.org/10.1007/978-3-319-90008-7

A.2   The Interview

The pioneer of object-orientation, co-designer of Smalltalk, and UI luminary opines on programming, browsers, objects, the illusion of patterns, and how Socrates could still make it to heaven.

By ANDREW BINSTOCK

In June of this year, the Association of Computing Machinery (ACM) celebrated the centenary of Alan Turing's birth by holding a conference with presentations by more than 30 Turing Award winners. The conference was filled with unusual lectures and panels [...] both about Turing and present-day computing. During a break in the proceedings, I interviewed Alan Kay—a Turing Award recipient known for many innovations and his articulated belief that the best way to predict the future is to invent it.[1]

Childhood as a Prodigy

Binstock:	*Let me start by asking you about a famous story. It states that you'd read more than 100 books by the time you went to first grade. This reading enabled you to realize that your teachers were frequently lying to you.*
Kay:	Yes, that story came out in a commemorative essay I was asked to write.
Binstock:	*So you're sitting there in first grade, and you're realizing that teachers are lying to you. Was that transformative? Did you all of a sudden view the whole world as populated by people who were dishonest?*
Kay:	Unless you're completely, certifiably insane, or a special kind of narcissist, you regard yourself as normal. So I didn't really think that much of it. I was basically an introverted type, and I was already following my own nose, and it was too late. I was just stubborn when they made me go along.
Binstock:	*So you called them on the lying.*

(continued)

---

[1]A side note: Re-creating Kay's answers to interview questions was particularly difficult. Rather than the linear explanation in response to an interview question, his answers were more of a cavalcade of topics, tangents, and tales threaded together, sometimes quite loosely—always rich, and frequently punctuated by strong opinions. The text that follows attempts to create somewhat more linearity to the content.—ALB.

Kay:	Yeah. But the thing that traumatized me occurred a couple years later, when I found an old copy of Life magazine that had the Margaret Bourke-White photos from Buchenwald. This was in the 1940s—no TV, living on a farm. That's when I realized that adults were dangerous. Like, really dangerous. I forgot about those pictures for a few years, but I had nightmares. But I had forgotten where the images came from. Seven or eight years later, I started getting memories back in snatches, and I went back and found the magazine. That probably was the turning point that changed my entire attitude toward life. It was responsible for getting me interested in education. My interest in education is unglamorous. I don't have an enormous desire to help children, but I have an enormous desire to create better adults.

The European Invasion in Computer Science

Kay:	You should talk to William Newman, since he's here. He was part of the British brain-drain. There was also Christopher Strachey, whom I consider one of the top 10 computer scientists of all time. The British appreciate him. They also had Peter Landin. They had memory management and they had timesharing before we did. Then there was a crisis in the early 1960s. And suddenly the young Brits were coming to the United States.
	William was one of the guys who literally wrote the book on computer graphics: Principles of Interactive Computer Graphics with Robert Sproull. William came to Harvard and was Ivan Sutherland's graduate student— got his Ph.D. in 1965 or 1966. William followed Ivan out to Utah; then when Xerox PARC was set up, William came to PARC.
	A similar thing happened, but I think for different reasons, in France. So one of the things we benefited from is that we got these incredibly well-prepared Brits and French guys reacting to the kind of devil-may-care attitude, and funding like nobody had ever seen before. These guys were huge contributors. For example, the first outline fonts were done by Patrick Baudelaire at PARC, who got his Ph.D. at Utah. The shading on 3D is named Gouraud shading after Henri Gouraud, who was also at Utah—also under Ivan, when Ivan was there.

Computing as Pop Culture

Binstock:	*You seem fastidious about always giving people credit for their work.*
Kay:	Well, I'm an old-fashioned guy. And I also happen to believe in history. The lack of interest, the disdain for history is what makes computing not-quite-a-field.
Binstock:	*You once referred to computing as pop culture.*
Kay:	It is. Complete pop culture. I'm not against pop culture. Developed music, for instance, needs a pop culture. There's a tendency to over-develop. Brahms and Dvorak needed gypsy music badly by the end of the nineteenth century. The big problem with our culture is that it's being dominated, because the electronic media we have is so much better suited for transmitting pop-culture content than it is for high-culture content. I consider jazz to be a developed part of high culture. Anything that's been worked on and developed and you [can] go to the next couple levels.
Binstock:	*One thing about jazz aficionados is that they take deep pleasure in knowing the history of jazz.*
Kay:	Yes! Classical music is like that, too. But pop culture holds a disdain for history. Pop culture is all about identity and feeling like you're participating. It has nothing to do with cooperation, the past or the future—it's living in the present. I think the same is true of most people who write code for money. They have no idea where [their culture came from]—and the Internet was done so well that most people think of it as a natural resource like the Pacific Ocean, rather than something that was man-made. When was the last time a technology with a scale like that was so error-free? The Web, in comparison, is a joke. The Web was done by amateurs.

The Browser: A Lament

Binstock:	*Still, you can't argue with the Web's success.*
Kay:	I think you can.
Binstock:	*Well, look at Wikipedia—it's a tremendous collaboration.*
Kay:	It is, but go to the article on Logo, can you write and execute Logo programs? Are there examples? No. The Wikipedia people didn't even imagine that, in spite of the fact that they're on a computer. That's why I never use PowerPoint. PowerPoint is just simulated acetate overhead slides, and to me, that is a kind of a moral crime.

(continued)

That's why I always do, not just dynamic stuff when I give a talk, but I do stuff that I'm interacting with on-the-fly. Because that is what the computer is for. People who don't do that either don't understand that or don't respect it.

The marketing people are not there to teach people, so probably one of the most disastrous interactions with computing was the fact that you could make money selling simulations of old, familiar media, and these apps just swamped most of the ideas of Doug Engelbart, for example. The Web browser, for many, many years, and still, even though it's running on a computer that can do X, Y, and Z, it's now up to about X and 1/2 of Y.

Binstock: *How do you mean?*

Kay: Go to a blog, go to any Wiki, and find one that's WYSIWYG like Microsoft Word is. Word was done in 1984. HyperCard was 1989. Find me Web pages that are even as good as HyperCard. The Web was done after that, but it was done by people who had no imagination. They were just trying to satisfy an immediate need. There's nothing wrong with that, except that when you have something like the Industrial Revolution squared, you wind up setting de facto standards—in this case, really bad de facto standards. Because what you definitely don't want in a Web browser is any features.

Binstock: *"Any features?"*

Kay: Yeah. You want to get those from the objects. You want it to be a mini-operating system, and the people who did the browser mistook it as an application. They flunked Operating Systems 101.

Binstock: *How so?*

Kay: I mean, look at it: The job of an operating system is to run arbitrary code safely. It's not there to tell you what kind of code you can run. Most operating systems have way too many features. The nice thing about UNIX when it was first done is not just that there were only 20 system commands, but the kernel was only about 1,000 lines of code. This is true of Linux also.

Binstock: *Yes.*

Kay: One of the ways of looking at it is the reason that WYSIWYG is slowly showing up in the browser is that it's a better way of interacting with the computer than the way they first did it. So of course they're going to reinvent it. I like to say that in the old days, if you reinvented the wheel, you would get your wrist slapped for not reading. But nowadays people are reinventing the flat tire. I'd personally be happy if they reinvented the wheel, because at least we'd be moving forward. If they reinvented what Engelbart did, we'd be way ahead of where we are now.

Objects

Kay: The flaw there is probably the fact that C is early-bound. Because it's not late-bound, because it's not a dynamic system, pretty much the only way you can link in features is to link them in ahead of time. Remember when we had to boot the computer? There's no need for that. There's never been any need for it. Because they did it that way, you wind up with megabytes of features that are essentially bundled together whether you want them or not. And now a thousand system calls, where what you really want is objects that are migrating around the net, and when you need a resource, it comes to you—no operating system. We didn't use an operating system at PARC. We didn't have applications either.

Binstock: *So it was just an object loader?*

Kay: An object exchanger, really. The user interface's job was to ask objects to show themselves and to composite those views with other ones.

Binstock: *You really radicalized the idea of objects by making everything in the system an object.*

Kay: No, I didn't. I mean, I made up the term "objects." Since we did objects first, there weren't any objects to radicalize. We started off with that view of objects, which is exactly the same as the view we had of what the Internet had to be, except in software. What happened was retrograde. When C++ came out, they tried to cater to C programmers, and they made a system that was neither fish nor fowl. And that's true of most of the things that are called object-oriented systems today. None of them are object-oriented systems according to my definition. Objects were a radical idea, then they got retrograded.

Binstock: *How do you view the Actor model?*

Kay: The first Smalltalk was presented at MIT, and Carl Hewitt and his folks, a few months later, wrote the first Actor paper. The difference between the two systems is that the Actor model retained more of what I thought were the good features of the object idea, whereas at PARC, we used Smalltalk to invent personal computing. It was actually a practical programming language as well as being interesting theoretically. I don't think there were too many practical systems done in Actors back then.

Programming

Binstock:	*Are you still programming?*
Kay:	I was never a great programmer. That's what got me into making more powerful programming languages. I do two kinds of programming. I do what you could call metaprogramming, and programming as children from the age of 9 to 13 or 14 would do. I spend a lot of time thinking about what children at those developmental levels can actually be powerful at, and what's the tradeoff between…Education is a double-edged sword. You have to start where people are, but if you stay there, you're not educating.
The most disastrous thing about programming—to pick one of the 10 most disastrous things about programming—there's a very popular movement based on pattern languages. When Christopher Alexander first did that in architecture, he was looking at 2,000 years of ways that humans have made themselves comfortable. So there was actually something to it, because he was dealing with a genome that hasn't changed that much. I think he got a few hundred valuable patterns out of it. But the bug in trying to do that in computing is the assumption that we know anything at all about programming. So extracting patterns from today's programming practices ennobles them in a way they don't deserve. It actually gives them more cachet. The best teacher I had in graduate school spent the whole semester destroying any beliefs we had about computing. He was a real iconoclast. He happened to be a genius, so we took it. At the end of the course, we were free because we didn't believe in anything. We had to learn everything, but then he destroyed it. He wanted us to understand what had been done, but he didn't want us to believe in it.
Binstock:	*Who was that?*
Kay:	That was Bob Barton, who was the designer of the Burroughs B5000. He's at the top of my list of people who should have received a Turing Award but didn't. The award is given by the Association for Computing Machinery (ACM), so that is ridiculous, but it represents the academic bias and software bias that the ACM has developed. It wasn't always that way. Barton was probably the number-one person who was alive who deserved it. He died last year, so it's not going to happen unless they go to posthumous awards.
Binstock:	*I don't think they do that.*
Kay:	They should. It's like the problem Christian religions have with how to get Socrates into heaven, right? You can't go to heaven unless you're baptized. If anyone deserves to go to heaven, it's Socrates, so this is a huge problem. But only the Mormons have solved this—and they did it. They proxy-baptized Socrates.

(continued)

Binstock:	*I didn't realize that. One can only imagine how thankful Socrates must be.*
Kay:	I thought it was pretty clever. It solves a thorny problem that the other churches haven't touched in 2,000 years.

Group Work

Kay:	Have you interviewed Vint Cerf?
Binstock:	*No.*
Kay:	He's a very special guy. Not just for brains. He's one of the better organizers of people. If you had to point to one person, given that the Internet was a community effort, the one who made that community work was Vint. And he also was the co-guy on TCP/IP. I love him. I've known him for years. He runs a pretty tough, pretty organized meeting, but he does it so well that everyone likes it.
	`[Digression on who, in addition to Cerf, should have` `won various computing prizes...]`
	The prizes aren't a thing that Dr. Dobb's worries about, because prizes are mostly for individuals, not for teams that are trying to do serious engineering projects. The dynamics are very different. A lot of people go into computing just because they are uncomfortable with other people. So it is no mean task to put together five different kinds of Asperger's syndrome and get them to cooperate. American business is completely fucked up because it is all about competition. Our world was built for the good from cooperation. That is what they should be teaching.
Binstock:	*That's one of the few redeeming things about athletics.*
Kay:	Absolutely! No question. Team sports. It's the closest analogy. Everyone has to play the game, but some people are better at certain aspects.

References

1. Achrekar, H., Gandhe, A., Lazarus, R., Yu, S.-H., & Liu, B. (2011). Predicting flu trends using twitter data. In *2011 IEEE Conference on Computer Communications Workshops (INFOCOM WKSHPS)* (pp. 702–707). New York: IEEE.
2. Aiello, M. (2017). *two bestsellers*. The Netherlands: Saccargia Holding BV Publisher.
3. Aiello, M., Monz, C., Todoran, L., & Worring, M. (2002). Document understanding for a broad class of documents. *International Journal of Document Analysis and Recognition, 5*(1), 1–16.
4. Aiello, M., Papazoglou, M., Yang, J., Carman, M., Pistore, M., Serafini, L., et al. (2002). A request language for web-services based on planning and constraint satisfaction. In *VLDB Workshop on Technologies for E-Services (TES)*. Lecture notes in computer science (pp. 76–85). Berlin: Springer.
5. Aiello, M., Zanoni, M., & Zolet, A. (2005). Exploring WS-notification: Building a scalable domotic infrastructure. *Dr. Dobb's Journal, 371*, 48–51.
6. Antoniou, G., & van Harmelen, F. (2004). *A semantic web primer*. Cambridge: MIT Press.
7. Asimov, I. (1950). *I, Robot*. New York: Spectra.
8. Baader, F., Calvanese, D., McGuinness, D. L., Nardi, D., & Patel-Schneider, P. F. (Eds.). (2003). *The description logic handbook: Theory, implementation and applications*. Cambridge: Cambridge University Press.
9. Bak, P. (1996). *How nature works: The science of self-organized criticality*. New York: Copurnicus.
10. Barabási, A.-L., & Albert, R. (1999). Emergence of scaling in random networks. *Science, 286*(5439), 509–512.
11. Barnes, S. B. (2003). ACM Turing Award biography. http://amturing.acm.org/award_winners/kay_3972189.cfm

© Springer International Publishing AG, part of Springer Nature 2018
M. Aiello, *The Web Was Done by Amateurs*,
https://doi.org/10.1007/978-3-319-90008-7

12. Barnett, R. (2013). *Web application defender's cookbook: Battling hackers and protecting users*. London: Wiley.
13. Barone, G., & Mocetti, S. (2016). What's your (sur)name? Intergenerational mobility over six centuries. http://voxeu.org/article/what-s-your-surname-intergenerational-mobility-over-six-centuries
14. Battelle, J. (2005). The birth of Google. *Wired, 13*(8), 108.
15. BBC News. Web's inventor gets a knighthood. http://news.bbc.co.uk/2/hi/technology/3357073.stm
16. BBC News. Creator of the web turns knight. http://news.bbc.co.uk/2/hi/technology/3899723.stm
17. Becchetti, L., & Castillo, C. (2006). The distribution of PageRank follows a power-law only for particular values of the damping factor. In *Proceedings of the 15th International Conference on World Wide Web* (pp. 941–942). New York: ACM.
18. Beck, M. T., Werner, M., Feld, S., & Schimper, T. (2014). Mobile edge computing: A taxonomy. In *Proceedings of the Sixth International Conference on Advances in Future Internet*. Citeseer.
19. Berners-Lee, T., & Fischetti, M. (1999). *Weaving the web: The original design and ultimate destiny of the world wide web by its inventor*. San Francisco: Harper.
20. Berners-Lee, T., Hendler, J., & Lassila, O. (2001). The semantic web. *Scientific American, 284*(5), 28–37.
21. Bianchini, M., Gori, M., & Scarselli, F. (2005). Inside pagerank. *ACM Transactions on Internet Technology, 5*(1), 92–128.
22. Bonomi, F., Milito, R., Zhu, J., & Addepalli, S. (2012). Fog computing and its role in the internet of things. In *Proceedings of the First Edition of the MCC Workshop on Mobile Cloud Computing* (pp. 13–16). New York: ACM.
23. Borges, J. L. (1962). The garden of forking paths. In *Collected fictions* (pp. 119–128). New York: Grove Press.
24. Bosch, A., Bogers, T., & Kunder, M. (2016). Estimating search engine index size variability: A 9-year longitudinal study. *Scientometrics, 107*(2), 839–856.
25. Bouguettaya, A., Singh, M., Huhns, M., Sheng, Q. Z., Dong, H., Yu, Q., et al. (2017). A service computing manifesto: The next 10 years. *Communications of the ACM, 60*(4), 64–72.
26. Brin, S., & Page, L. (1998). The anatomy of a large-scale hypertextual web search engine. *Computer Networks and ISDN Systems, 30*(1), 107–117.
27. Broder, A. Z., Kumar, R., Maghoul, F., Raghavan, P., Rajagopalan, S., Stata, R., et al. (2000). Graph structure in the web. *Computer Networks, 33*(1–6), 309–320.
28. Brown, M. H., & Najork, M. A. (1996). Distributed active objects. *Computer Networks and ISDN Systems, 28*(7), 1037–1052. Proceedings of the Fifth International World Wide Web Conference 6–10 May 1996.
29. Bush, V. (1945). As we may think. *Atlantic Monthly, 176*, 101–108.
30. Calvino, I. (2010). *The castle of crossed destinies*. New York: Random House.
31. Camden, R. (2015). *Client-side data storage*. Sebastopol: O'Reilly.

32. Campbell, M., Hoane, A. J., & Hsu, F.-H. (2002). Deep blue. *Artificial Intelligence, 134*(1–2), 57–83 (2002).
33. Cardelli, L. (1995). A language with distributed scope. In *Proceedings of the 22nd ACM SIGPLAN-SIGACT Symposium on Principles of Programming Languages* (pp. 286–297). New York: ACM.
34. Cerf, V. G., & Kahn, R. E. (1974). A protocol for packet network intercommunication. *IEEE Transactions on Communication, 22*(5), 637–648.
35. Cerf, V. G., & Kahn, R. E. (2005). A protocol for packet network intercommunication. *ACM SIGCOMM Computer Communication Review, 35*(2), 71–82.
36. Chaffey, D. (2017, March). Mobile marketing statistics compilation. Technical report, Smart Insights. http://www.smartinsights.com/mobile-marketing/mobile-marketing-analytics/mobile-marketing-statistics/
37. Chappell, D. (2004). *Enterprise service bus.* Sebastopol: O'Reilly Media, Inc.
38. Chen, F., Chen, Z., Wang, X., & Yuan, Z. (2008). The average path length of scale free networks. *Communications in Nonlinear Science and Numerical Simulation, 13*(7), 1405–1410.
39. Codd, E. F. (1970). A relational model of data for large shared data banks. *Communications of the ACM, 13*(6), 377–387.
40. Computer Museum. (2017). DEC PDP-1. http://www.computermuseum.li/Testpage/DEC-PDP1-1960.htm
41. Conklin, J. (1987). Hypertext: A survey and introduction. *Computer, 20*(9), 17–41.
42. Coulouris, G., Dollimore, J., Kindberg, T., & Blair, G. (2011). *Distributed systems: Concepts and design.* Reading: Addison-Wesley.
43. Dever, J. (1984). *Lone Wolf. Flight from the dark.* Boston: Sparrow Books.
44. Donini, F. M., Lenzerini, M., Nardi, D., & Nutt, W. (1991). Tractable concept languages. In *Proceedings of the 12th International Joint Conference on Artificial Intelligence* (Vol. 91, pp. 458–463).
45. Edwards, O. (1997, August 25). Ted Nelson. *Forbes.*
46. Engelbart, D. C. (1962). Augmenting human intellect: A conceptual framework. Technical Report Summary Report AFOSR-3223, Stanford Research Institute.
47. Fall, K. R., & Stevens, W. R. (2011). *TCP/IP illustrated, volume 1: The protocols.* Reading: Addison-Wesley.
48. Fielding, R. T. (2000). *Architectural styles and the design of network-based software architectures.* PhD thesis, University of California, Irvine.
49. Fitzgerald, M. (2008, May 25). Cloud computing: So you don't have to stand still. http://www.nytimes.com/2008/05/25/technology/25proto.html
50. Franceschet, M. (2011). PageRank: Standing on the shoulders of giants. *Communications of the ACM, 54*(6), 92–101.
51. Garcia Lopez, P., Montresor, A., Epema, D., Datta, A., Higashino, T., Iamnitchi, A., et al. (2015). Edge-centric computing: Vision and challenges. *ACM SIGCOMM Computer Communication Review, 45*(5), 37–42.

52. Garrett, J. J. (2005). Ajax: A new approach to web applications. http://adaptivepath.org/ideas/ajax-new-approach-web-applications/

53. Geddes, M. How far can the Internet scale? http://www.martingeddes.com/how-far-can-the-internet-scale/

54. Georgievski, I., & Aiello, M. (2015). HTN planning: Overview, comparison, and beyond. *Artificial Intelligence, 222*, 124–156.

55. Ghallab, M., Nau, D., & Traverso, P. (2004). *Automated planning: Theory and practice*. Burlington: Morgan Kaufmann.

56. Gray, M. (1995). Measuring the growth of the web: June 1993 to June 1995. http://www.mit.edu/people/mkgray/growth

57. Green, J. L., & Peters, D. J. (1985). Introduction to the space physics analysis network (span). Technical Report NASA-TM-86499, NAS 1.15:86499, NASA.

58. Hafner, K., & Lyon, M. (1996). *Where wizards stay up late: The origins of the Internet* (1st ed.). New York: Simon & Schuster.

59. Hayes, B. (2008). Cloud computing. *Communications of the ACM, 51*(7), 9–11.

60. Henning, M. (2008). The rise and fall of CORBA. *Communication of the ACM, 51*(8), 53–57.

61. History of Computer: TCP/IP. http://www.history-computer.com/Internet/Maturing/TCPIP.html

62. IETF and ISOC. RFC official repository. https://www.rfc-editor.org/

63. Internet Society. Brief history of the Internet. http://www.internetsociety.org/internet/what-internet/history-internet/brief-history-internet

64. Isaacson, W. (2014). *The innovators. How a group of hackers, geniuses and geeks created the digital revolution*. New York: Simon & Schuster.

65. Kaldeli, E., Lazovik, A., & Aiello, M. (2016). Domain-independent planning for services in uncertain and dynamic environments. *Artificial Intelligence, 236*(7), 30–64 (2016).

66. Kaldeli, E., Warriach, E., Lazovik, A., & Aiello, M. (2013). Coordinating the web of services for a smart home. *ACM Transactions on the Web, 7(2)*, 10.

67. Kapur, A. (2017, February 22). Mobile apps vs. mobile web: Do you have to choose?. https://www.business.com/articles/mobile-apps-vs-mobile-web-do-you-have-to-choose/

68. Kay, A. C. (1972) A personal computer for children of all ages. In *Proceedings of the ACM Annual Conference-Volume 1* (p. 1). New York: ACM.

69. Kleinberg, J. M., Kumar, R., Raghavan, P., Rajagopalan, S., & Tomkins, A. S. (1999). *The web as a graph: Measurements, models, and methods* (pp. 1–17). Berlin: Springer.

70. Knoblock, C. A., Minton, S., Ambite, J.-L., Ashish, N., Muslea, I., Philpot, A. G., et al. (2001). The Ariadne approach to web-based information integration. *International the Journal on Cooperative Information Systems, 10*(1–2), 145–169 (2001).

71. Kristol, D. M. (2001). Http cookies: Standards, privacy, and politics. *ACM Transactions on Internet Technology, 1*(2), 151–198.

72. Kuhn, T. (1962). *The structure of scientific revolutions*. Chicago: University of Chicago Press.

73. LaMonica, M. (2004, September). Sarvega brings routing to XML. https://www.cnet.com/au/news/sarvega-brings-routing-to-xml/

74. Langville, A. N., & Meyer, C. D. (2006) *Google's PageRank and beyond: The science of search engine rankings*. Princeton: Princeton University Press.

75. Laporte, L. (2016, April 25). Triangulation 247 interview with Bill Atkinson. https://twit.tv/shows/triangulation/episodes/247

76. Lazer, D., Kennedy, R., King, G., & Vespignani, A. (2014). The parable of Google Flu: Traps in big data analysis. *Science, 343*(6176), 1203–1205.

77. Lazovik, A., Aiello, M., & Papazoglou, M. (2003). Planning and monitoring the execution of Web service requests. In *Proceedings of the 1st International Conference on Service-Oriented Computing (ICSOC)* (pp. 335–350). Berlin: Springer.

78. Lazovik, A., Aiello, M., & Papazoglou, M. (2006). Planning and monitoring the execution of Web service requests. *Journal on Digital Libraries, 6*(3), 235–246.

79. Leontief, W. W. (1941). *Structure of American economy, 1919–1929*. Cambridge: Harvard University Press.

80. Licklider, J. (1960). Man-computer symbiosis. *IRE Transactions on Human Factors in Electronics, 1*, 4–11.

81. Licklider, J. (1963, April 23). Memorandum for: Members and affiliates of the intergalactic computer network. Technical Report, ARPA.

82. Limer, E. (2014). My brief and curious life as a Mechanical Turk. http://gizmodo.com/

83. Lubbers, P., & Greco, F. (2010). HTML5 Web sockets: A quantum leap in scalability for the Web. *SOA World Magazine, (1)*.

84. Lyons, D. A. (2012). Net neutrality and nondiscrimination norms in telecommunications. *Arizona Law Review, 54*, 1029.

85. Manning, R. (2004, May 20). Dynamic and distributed managed edge computing (Mec) framework. US Patent App. 10/850,291.

86. McDermott, D. (2002). Estimated-regression planning for interactions with Web Services. In *6th International Conference on AI Planning and Scheduling*. Palo Alto: AAAI Press.

87. McIlarth, S., & Son, T. C. (2002). Adapting Golog for composition of semantic web-services. In *Proceedings of the 8th International Conference on Principles of Knowledge Representation and Reasoning (KR)* (pp. 482–496). Burlington: Morgan Kaufmann.

88. Milgram, S. (1967). The small world problem. *Psychology Today, 1*, 61–67.

89. Mims, C. (2014, November 17). The web is dying; apps are killing it. *Wall Street Journal*.

90. Minkowski, M. S., & Powell, J. C. (2014). *Single page web applications*. Shelter Island: Manning.

91. Nelson, T. H. (1965). Complex information processing: A file structure for the complex, the changing and the indeterminate. In *Proceedings of the 1965 20th National Conference* (pp. 84–100). New York: ACM.

92. Nelson, T. H. (1980). *Literary machines 93.1.: The report on, and of, project Xanadu concerning word processing, electronic publishing, hypertext, thinkertoys, tomorrow's intellectual revolution, and certain other topics including knowledge, education and freedom (1993 Edition)*. Sausalito: Mindful Press.

93. Nelson, T. H. (2007, May 17). Intertwingularity: When ideas collide uploaded. Ted Nelson's 70th Birthday Lecture.

94. Newman, M. E. J. (2003). The structure and function of complex networks. *SIAM Review, 45*(2), 167–256.

95. Pagani, G. A., & Aiello, M. (2013). The power grid as a complex network: A survey. *Physica A: Statistical Mechanics and Its Applications, 392*(1), 2688–2700.

96. Papazoglou, M. (2008). *Web services: Principles and technology*. London: Pearson Education.

97. Papazoglou, M., & Georgakopoulos, D. (2003). Service-oriented computing. *Communications of the ACM, 46*(10), 24–28.

98. Philp, R. K. (1865). *Enquire within upon everything*. London: Houlston and Wright.

99. Pinski, G., & Narin, F. (1976). Citation influence for journal aggregates of scientific publications: Theory, with application to the literature of physics. *Information Processing & Management, 12*(5), 297–312.

100. Raymond, E. S. (1996). *The new hacker's dictionary*. Cambridge: MIT Press.

101. Saltzer, J. H., Reed, D. P., & Clark, D. D. (1984). End-to-end arguments in system design. *ACM Transactions on Computer Systems, 2*(4), 277–288.

102. Seeley, J. R. (1949). The net of reciprocal influence. A problem in treating sociometric data. *Canadian Journal of Experimental Psychology, 3*, 234.

103. Seetharaman, K. (1998). The CORBA connection - Introduction to the CORBA special issue. *Communications of the ACM, 41*(10), 34–36.

104. Segal, B. (1985). A short history of Internet protocols at CERN. http://ben.web.cern.ch/ben/TCPHIST.html

105. Sink, E. Memories from the browser wars. http://ericsink.com/Browser_Wars.html

106. Spohrer, J., Maglio, P. P., Bailey, J., & Gruhl, D. (2007). Steps toward a science of service systems. *Computer, 40*(1), 71–77.

107. Stuttard, D., & Pinto, M. (2011). *The web application hacker's handbook* (2nd ed.). London: Wiley.

108. Tilley, S. (1999). The need for speed. *Communication of the ACM, 42*(7), 23–26.

109. Travers, J., & Milgram, S. (1969). An experimental study of the small world problem. *Sociometry, 32*(4), 425–443.

110. Turing, A. M. (1950). Computing machinery and intelligence. *Mind, 59*(236), 433–460.

111. van Benthem, J. (1983). *The logic of time*. London: Reidel.

112. Various Authors. (2005). InnoQ's web services standards poster, version 2.0.
113. Various Authors. HTML 5 test. http://www.html5test.com
114. Varshney, U., Snow, A., McGivern, M., & Howard, C. (2002). Voice over IP. *Communication of the ACM, 45*(1), 89–96.
115. Vise, D. (2007). The Google story. *Strategic Direction, 23*(10), 192–199.
116. Vogels, W. (2001, January). How and why did amazon get into the cloud computing business? https://www.quora.com/How-and-why-did-Amazon-get-into-the-cloud-computing-business
117. Waldrop, M. (2001) *The dream machine: JCR Licklider and the revolution that made computing personal.* New York: Viking Penguin.
118. Watts, D. J., & Strogatz, S. H. (1998). Collective dynamics of 'small-world' networks. *Nature, 393*(6684), 440–442.
119. Weiser, M. (1991). The computer for the 21st century. *Scientific American, 265*(3), 94–104.
120. Witten, I. H., Gori, M., & Numerico, T. (2010). *Web dragons: Inside the myths of search engine technology.* Amsterdam: Elsevier.
121. Wolf, G. (1995). The curse of Xanadu. *Wired Magazine, 3*, 137–202.
122. Woods, W. A. (1975). What's in a link: Foundations for semantic networks. In *Representation and understanding: Studies in cognitive science* (pp. 35–82). New York: Academic.
123. Woollaston, V. (March 2014). How the web was described when Berners-Lee proposed the concept to his boss 25 years ago today.
124. Wu, T. (2003). Network neutrality, broadband discrimination. *Journal on Telecommunications and High Technology Law, 2*, 141–176.
125. Zimmermann, H. (1980). OSI reference model–The ISO model of architecture for open systems interconnection. *IEEE Transactions on communications, 28*(4), 425–432.

Index

Abhay Bhushan, 14
ACM Turing Award, 2, 5, 146, 151
Act One, 17
Active Endpoints, 94
Adobe, 94, 126
Advanced Research Projects Agency. *see*
    DARPA
AJAX, 3, 75
Alan Emtage, 123
Alan Kay, x, 1–5, 9, 18, 32, 38, 41, 51,
    52, 60, 65, 77, 82, 91, 95,
    111, 130, 133, 134, 141, 143,
    146–152
Alan Turing, 27, 137, 146
    Turing machine, 89
    Turing test, 137, 139
Albert Einstein, vii
Albert-Laszló Barabasi, 120
Alexander Lazovik, 87, 139
Aliweb, 123
AlphaGo, 137
Altavista, 124
Amazon, 35, 92, 93, 96, 97, 132
    AWS, 93, 97
    Turk, 93
Amazon Web Services. *see* AWS

American Appliances Company, 25
American OnLine, 57
Andrew Binstock, 1, 146, 148–152
Animoto, 97
APIs, 92
APL, 120
Apple, 2, 32, 34, 36, 131, 133
    App Store, 131
    iOS, 132
    Macintosh, 2, 34
    Safari, 60
Applet, 52, 71
Application Programmable Interfaces.
    see APIs
apps, 130
Archie, 123
architecture
    client-server, 32, 42, 43, 65, 68–70,
        76, 83, 94, 98, 142
    n-tier, 43
    three-tier, 43, 80, 135
ARPA. *see* DARPA
ARPANET, 2, 9, 10, 12–17, 34, 42, 141
Artificial Intelligence, vii, 11, 27, 92,
        134, 136–138
    Planning, 87, 90, 91, 136

© Springer International Publishing AG, part of Springer Nature 2018
M. Aiello, *The Web Was Done by Amateurs*,
https://doi.org/10.1007/978-3-319-90008-7

Ask Geeves, 117
Asynchronous JavaScript+XML. *see*
    AJAX
AT&T, 18
average path length. *see* APL
AWS, 97

BackRub, 124
Baidu, 121
BBN, 12
BEA, 94
Berkeley University, 28, 55
Big Data, 110, 138
Bill Atkinson, 32, 33
Bill Gates, 59, 79, 83, 129
binary tree, 24
Bing, 117
Bluetooth, 133
Bob Kahn, 12, 14, 20
Bob Taylor, 11
Bolt Baranek and Newman. *see* BBN
bow-tie model, 118, 119
BPEL, 88, 89
BPEL4People, 94
Brad Rutter, 136
Brendan Eich, 73
British National Physical Laboratory. *see*
    NPL
Brown University, 127
browser wars, 6, 51, 57, 60, 65, 73

Carl Jung, vii
Cascading Style Sheets. *see* CSS
CERN, 4, 33–37, 48, 53, 55, 101, 109,
    116, 136
CGI, 69, 70
chain, 23
characteristic path length. *see* CPL
Chrome, 60, 61, 76
Cisco, 98
Cloud Computing, 96, 97

Cloudlet, 98
clustering coefficient, 119
Common Gateway Interfaces. *see* CGI
Common Object Request Broker
    Architecture. *see* CORBA
computer mouse, 28
cookies, 3, 56, 65, 68, 73, 77, 126
copying model, 121
CORBA, 50, 79–82, 85
Cornell, 96, 123
corporate continent, 118
CPL, 120, 121
crawler, 116, 117, 123
CSNET, 16
CSS, 66
CWI, 35, 89

DAG, 24
DAML, 105, 109
Dan Libby, 76
DARPA, 10, 11, 17, 37, 105, 109
    Grand Challenge, 137
DARPA Machine Markup Language.
    see DAML
datagram, 15
DataPower, 95
Dave Winer, 76
Dave Farber, 16
David Chappell, 95
David Clark, 126
David Reed, 126
DCNET, 16
deep packet inspection, 20
Defence Advance Research Project
    Agency. *see* DARPA
description logics, 105, 107
Dew Computing, 98
Digital Equipment, 16
Dimitri Georgakopoulus, 87
directed acyclic graphs. *see* DAG
DNS, 46, 96
DNSSEC, 143

DoD Standard Internet Protocol. *see* IP
Domain Name System. *see* DNS
Domain Name System Security
       Extension. *see* DNSSEC
Donald Knuth, 5, 49
Donald Watts Davis, 11
Dorothy Robling Denning, 16
Douglas Crockford, 75
Douglas Engelbart, 2, 5, 12, 28, 29, 32,
       37, 51, 134, 136, 149
Dr. Dobb's journal, 1, 145, 146
Dropbox, 97
Duncan Watts, 119
DynaBook, 41, 134
dynamic service composition, 90

eBay, 92, 95
EC2, 97
Edgar Codd, 5, 38
Edge Computing, 72, 98, 136
Elastic Compute Cloud. *see* EC2
end-to-end argument, 126
Enquire, 34–38
Enrico Fermi, vii
Enterprise Service Bus. *see* ESB
Eric Bina, 55
Erik Sink, 57
ESB, 95
European Commission, 37, 105, 109
       Seventh Framework, 110
       Sixth Framework, 110
European Organization for Nuclear
       Research. *see* CERN
Excite, 123
eXtensible Markup Language. *see* XML

Facebook, 35, 93, 97, 121, 132
Faris Nizamic, 139
fat client, 72, 97
Fermilab, 116
Ferranti Mark 1, 33

Ferrari, 119
File Transfer Protocol. *see* FTP
Firefox, 60
firewall, 80
First Browser War, 57, 60
first-order logic, 105, 107
Flash, 76, 126
Flurry analytics, 132
Fog Computing, 98
Frank Leymann, 83
Franklin Delano Roosevelt, 26
FTP, 14, 36, 37, 123

Gary Kasparov, 93, 137
Gateway, 15
Generalized Markup Language. *see*
       GML
generic graph, 24
Gerard Salton, 123
GML, 48
Google, 3, 6, 35, 60, 75, 76, 110, 115,
       117, 121, 124, 133
       Android, 132
       bomb, 125, 142
       Google Play, 131
Gopher, 127
Grid/Mesh Computing, 98

Harvard, 119, 123, 147
HEPNet, 16
Herman Melville, 66, 67, 69, 103
Honeywell DDP-516, 12
HTML, 4, 5, 18, 36, 37, 41, 44, 48–50,
       52, 53, 60, 68–71, 73–76, 92,
       101, 102, 110, 111, 122, 123, 132,
       133, 142, 159
HTTP, 4, 36, 37, 44, 46–48, 66, 68,
       74–76, 79, 80, 82, 84, 94, 95,
       132, 133
       GET, 46
       POST, 46

HyperCard, 32, 33, 35, 51, 65, 111, 127, 142, 149
hypermedia, 24, 25, 27, 33, 38, 143
hyperreference, 23
HyperTalk, 33
hypertext, 4, 22–24, 29, 30, 33, 35, 37, 93, 102, 110, 111, 127, 143
HyperText Markup Language. *see* HTML
HyperText Transfer Protocol. *see* HTTP

IaaS, 96
IBM, 2, 11, 18, 38, 48, 83, 93–96, 126, 129
    Deep Blue, 93, 137
    Watson, 109, 136
ICSOC, 94
ICWS, 95
IDL, 82, 85, 92
IETF, 13, 37, 76
IMP, 11, 12, 14, 15, 18
Information Retrieval, 4, 110, 123, 138
Infoseek, 123
Infrastructure as a Service. *see* IaaS
InPerFor, 119
Intel, 98
Interface Definition Language. *see* IDL
Interface Message Processors. *see* IMP
Intergalactic Network, 11
Intermedia, 127
Internet Engineering Task Force. *see* IETF
Internet Explorer, 57, 59–61, 73, 75
Internet of Things. *see* IoT
Internet Society. *see* ISOC
intertwingularity, 29
Intranet, 80
IoT, 98, 134
IP, 15, 17, 46
Isaac Asimov, 139, 140
    three laws of robotics, 139
ISO/OSI model, 127

ISOC, 13
Italo Calvino, 22

Jack Ruina, 10
James Gosling, 71
James Hendler, 105
Janet, 16
Java, 70–73, 77, 81, 85, 88, 126
Java Virtual Machine. *see* JVM
JavaScript, 3, 73–75, 77, 142
    JSON, 74, 75, 95
    Single Page Application, 75
JavaScript Object Notation. *see* JSON
Jeff Conklin, 32
Jeopardy!, 109, 136
Jerry Saltzer, 126
Jesse James Garrett, 75
Jini, 85
Joe Dever, 24
John Gage, 72
John McCarthy, 2, 5, 27, 137
John Postel, 15, 17, 42
    Postel Law, 15
Jorge Luis Borges, 21
Joseph Carl Robnett Licklider, 10, 11
JSON, 75
JVM, 71, 72, 77, 85

Kempinski Hotels, 97
Ken Jennings, 136
Krishnan Seetharaman, 81

Larry Landweber, 16
Larry Page, 124
last mile problem, 18
LaTeX, 49, 73
Lego, 89–91
Leonid Leontief, 124
Leslie Lamport, 5, 17, 49
LinkedIn, 93

LiveScript, 73
Logo, 4, 52, 102
Louis Montulli, 68
Lynx, 53, 68

Manhattan Project, 26
Marc Andreessen, 55
Marco Gori, 125
Mark Weiser, 41, 134, 136
Marshall Space Flight Center, 16
Martijn Koster, 123
Martin Haeberli, 127
Matthew Gray, 117
Maurizio Lenzerini, 107
McGill University, 123
Mechanical Turk. *see* Amazon
Memex, 26–28
MFENet, 16
Michi Henning, 82
microfilm, 25, 26
Microsoft, 6, 57–59, 73, 75, 86, 96, 98,
        125, 126, 129, 133
    Windows mobile, 132
    Windows store, 131
Mike Papazoglou, 87, 90
Mike Sendall, 35
Milgram continent, 118
MIME, 133
MIT, 12, 14, 25, 117, 126, 150
Moby Dick, 46–48, 67, 69, 103, 106,
        115
modal logics, 107
Mosaic, 55, 56, 58, 61
Mozilla FireFox, 59

NACA, 10
NASA, 10, 26, 29
Nathan Sawaya, 89
National Advisory Committee for
        Aeronautics. *see* NACA

National Aeronautics and Space
        Administration. *see* NASA
National Center for Supercomputing
        Applications. *see* NCSA
NCP, 14, 17
NCSA, 5, 55, 56, 69, 116
Net neutrality, 6, 20
Netflix, 97
Netscape, 6, 56–60, 65, 68, 73, 76, 124,
        126, 127, 142
    Mozilla, 57, 59
Network Control Program. *see* NCP
new archipelago, 118
NeXT, 36, 53
NFC, 133
Nikhef, 116
NLS, 2, 15, 29, 32, 42
NPL, 11

OASIS, 96
Objective-C, 36
Oblets, 111
Obliq, 111
Ohio State University, 116
OIL, 105, 109
oN-Line System. *see* NLS
ontology, 34, 102–105, 110
Ontology Inference Layer. *see* OIL
Ontology Web Languages. *see* OWL
OpenFog, 98
Oracle, 94
OTHERwise, 55
OWL, 105, 107, 109, 111
    DL, 105, 107
    Full, 105
    Lite, 105, 107
Oxford University, 33

PaaS, 96
PageRank, 124, 125, 142
paradigm shifts, 128

PARC, 2, 41, 42, 134, 147, 150
Pareto law, 120
patch, 3, 52, 65, 66, 69, 73, 76, 77, 79,
        86, 92, 93, 98, 108–110, 122,
        126, 132, 133, 136, 141–143
    cookies, 66
    Java, 69
    Javascript, 73
    scripting, 73
    Semantic Web, 108
    Web Services, 86
pattern
    publish-find-bind, 79, 84–87
    Web pattern, 44, 122, 126, 127
PDF, 133
PDP-1, 41
Pei-Yuan Wei, 55, 129
Per Bak, 127, 128
Pervasive Computing, 85, 134
Platform as a Service. *see* PaaS
Postel Law. *see* John Postel
preferential attachment model, 120, 121
Printers Inc., 71
private jet, 109
publish-find-bind. *see* pattern
Purdue University, 16

Réka Albert, 120
Ramanathan V. Guha, 76
RAND, 11
Raymond Almiran Montgomery, 24
Raython, 25
RDF, 76, 103–105, 109–111
    schema, 103
RDFS, 103–105
reification, 104, 105
Representational State Transfer. *see*
        REST
Request for Comments. *see* RFC
Resource Description Framework. *see*
        RDF
REST, 94, 95, 97

JSON, 95
RFC, 12–17, 42, 46, 47, 49, 68, 76
Robert E. Kahn, 5
Roy Fielding, 94
RSS, 76
RuGCo planner, 91

S3, 97
SaaS, 96
SAGE, 10
sandboxing, 72, 132
SAP, 94, 96, 126
Sarvega, 95
Scalable Vector Graphics. *see* SVG
scale-free, 18, 24, 120, 121, 124
Secure Socket Layer. *see* SSL
semantic networks, 107
Semantic Web, 34, 101–103, 105–111,
        127, 129
    reasoning, 106
Semi-Automatic Ground Environment.
        see SAGE
Sergei Brin, 124
Service Science, 93
Service-Oriented Computing. *see* SOC
serving-host, 42
SGML, 48–50
Sigmund Freud, vii
Silverlight, 126
Simple Queue Service. *see* SQS
Simple Storage Service. *see* S3
Simple-Object Access Protocol. *see*
        SOAP
SLAC, 37, 116
Small-World model, 119
SmallTalk, 2, 111, 134, 150
SMART, 123
smart spaces, 134
SNMP, 83
SOAP, 3, 82–84, 87, 89, 94, 97
SOC, 87, 92–94, 96
Software as a Service. *see* SaaS

SPAN, 16
Specification of Internet Transmission
    Control Program. *see* TCP
spider, 116
Spyglass, 57–59
SQS, 97
SRI, 12, 15, 28, 42
SSL, 56, 65, 142
Standard for the Transmission of IP
    Datagrams on Avia, 15
Standard Generalized Markup
    Language. *see* SGML
Stanford, 14, 116, 123, 124
Stanford Linear Accelerator Center. *see*
    SLAC
Stanley Kubrick, 1, 139
Stanley Milgram, 119
Steve Jobs, 36
Steven Strogatz, 119
subsumption, 106
Sun Microsystems, 69–73, 126
SunSite, 116
SustainableBuildings, 139
SVG, 66
System for the Mechanical Analysis and
    Retrieval of Text. *see* SMART

tarock, 23
TCP, 14–20, 44, 46, 152
TCP/IP. *see* TCP
TCPConnection, 76
Ted Nelson, x, 4, 5, 24, 29–32, 35, 37,
    136
terra incognita, 118
Terry Winograd, 124
The Mother of All Demos, 2, 29, 37
The Mother of All Patches, 108
thin client, 72
Thomas J. Watson, 129
Thomas Kuhn, 128
Thomas Reardon, 57
three-tier architecture, 43

Tim Berners-Lee, viii, x, 4–6, 9, 20,
    33–38, 44, 46, 49, 52–55, 59,
    101, 102, 105, 111, 116, 129, 132,
    136
Tim Wu, 20
transclusions, 4, 29–31
Trigg's Textnet, 127
Tuan Anh Nguyen, 139
Tufts, 25
Twitter, 115
two-variable guarded fragment, 107

Ubiquitous Computing, 41, 134
UBR, 96
UCLA, 12, 14, 15, 17, 42
UDDI, 83, 84, 88–90, 96
UDP, 15, 46
Uniform Resource Locators. *see* URL
Universal Business Registry. *see* UBR
Universal Description, Discovery, and
    Integration. *see* UDDI
Universal Plug and Play, 86, 102
University of California, Irvine, 94
University of Colorado, 2
University of Illinois, 55
University of Santa Barbara, 12
University of Texas at Dallas, 16
University of Trento, 87
University of Utah, 2, 12, 41, 147
UPnP, 85, 86, 102, 103
URI, 37, 45, 47
URL, 4, 43–48, 68, 83, 117, 122, 123
User Datagram Protocol. *see* UDP
Utah State University, 16

Vannevar Bush, 25–29, 37
Venky Harinarayan, 93
Vilfredo Pareto, 121
    law, 120
Vinton G. Cerf, 5, 14, 15, 17, 18, 20, 152
Viola, 55

Visual Basic Scripting, 73
Vordel, 95
Vrije Universiteit Amsterdam, 96

W3C, 37, 103, 105, 125
Web graph, 23, 44, 124, 125
Web pattern, 44
Web Search Engines, 122
Web Service Business Process Execution
    Language. *see* BPEL
Web Service Description Language. *see*
    WSDL
Web Service Flow Language. *see* WSFL
Web Services, 79, 83–85, 88, 89, 91–96,
    126
  REST, 94
  standards, 87
WebSockets, 76
Werner Vogels, 96
whale, 4, 46–48, 60, 69, 70, 74, 103,
    105, 106
  sperm, 46, 48, 66, 67, 74, 106
What You See Is What You Get. *see*
    WYSIWYG
Wikipedia, x, 4, 121, 148, 149
Wolfgang von Kempelen, 93
World Wide Web Wanderer, 117
World Wide Web Consortium. *see*
    W3C

WorldWideWeb, 36, 53
WS-HumanTask, 94
WS-Security, 83
WSDL, 3, 83, 84, 87–90, 93, 94
WSFL, 83
WYSIWYG, 49, 149
WYSopIWYG, 53

X.25, 16
Xanadu, x, 4, 29–32, 127
  requirements, 31
XEROX Palo Alto Research Center. *see*
    PARC
XML, 50, 75, 82, 83, 86, 88, 91, 92, 94,
    95, 97, 102, 103, 105
  router, 95
  Web Services, 94
XMLHttpRequest, 75, 76, 126

Yahoo!, 117, 122, 123, 132
YouTube, 121

ZigBee, 133
ZigZag, 29
zippered lists, 29

Printed in the United States
By Bookmasters